Soho Theatre Company presents

Blue Eyes & Heels

by Toby Whithouse

First performed at Soho Theatre on 12 October 2005

Soho Theatre is supported by

 gettyimages | TEQUILA\ | **Bloomberg**

LONDON

Performances in the Lorenz Auditorium

Registered Charity No: 267234

Soho Theatre Company presents

Blue Eyes & Heels

by Toby Whithouse

Serena Evans	Emma
Martin Freeman	Duncan
John Stahl	Victor

Director	Jonathan Lloyd
Designer	Jonathan Fensom
Lighting Designer	Jason Taylor
Sound Designer	Matt McKenzie
Assistant Director	Leann O'Kasi
Casting	Ginny Schiller
Costume Supervisor	Jane Gooday
Fight Director	Mikey Whiplash

Production Manager	Nick Ferguson
Stage Manager	Sarah Buik
Assistant Stage Manager	Geraldine Mullins
Chief Technician	Nick Blount
Chief Electrician	Christoph Wagner
Lighting Technician	Mark Watts
Scenery built and painted by	Robert Knight Ltd

Press Representation	Nancy Poole (020 7478 0142)
Photography	Getty Images

Soho Theatre Company would like to thank:

Brian Dixon at All Star Wrestling, Emma Wilson, Technical Manager at Sadlers Wells

Writer

Toby Whithouse Writer

Toby's first play *Jump Mr Malinoff, Jump* won the 1998 Verity Bargate award. It was the opening production at Soho Theatre in 2000, and has since been adapted for radio. For television he has written on *Where The Heart Is*, *Attachments*, *Doctor Who*, *Hotel Babylon* and devised the series *No Angels*.

Cast

Serena Evans Emma

Serena's theatre credits include *Candida* (Oxford Stage Company); *Life x 3* (Savoy Theatre); *The Constant Wife* (Apollo Theatre); *A Small Family Business* (Chichester Festival Theatre); *Remember This* (RNT); *Things We Do For Love* (Gielgud Theatre); *A Midsummer Night's Dream* (Open Air Theatre, Regent's Park); *Love For Love* (Chichester Festival Theatre); *The Killing Of Sister George* (Ambassadors Theatre); *Lysistrata* (Liverpool & Old Vic); *The Comedy Of Errors* (RSC); *The Recruiting Officer* (RNT); *Confusions, Calling and Blithe Spirit* (all at Stephen Joseph Theatre, Scarborough); *The Norman Conquests* (Thorndike Theatre); *Getting On* (Palace Theatre, Watford); *Candlelight* (Palace Theatre, Watford); *Henceforward* (Stephen Joseph Theatre, Scarborough and Vaudeville Theatre) – SWET Award Nomination for Best Supporting Actress; *Time And Time Again* (UK & Canadian Tour); *Charley's Aunt* (Birmingham Rep); *Noises Off* (Savoy Theatre). Television credits include Sergeant Dawkins in *The Thin Blue Line* (BBC), *Trial And Retribution* (LaPlante Productions); *Every Woman Knows A Secret* (Carnival); *Ruth Rendell Mystery – You Can't Be Too Careful* (Blue Heaven); *Pie In The Sky* (SelecTV); *Came Out, It Rained, Went Back In Again* (BBC); *The Piglet Files* – 3 series (LWT); *The Management* (LWT); *Never Come Back* (BBC); *Mr Majeika* (TVS), *The Comic Strip Presents* series.

Martin Freeman Duncan

Martin's theatre credits include *Kosher Harry* (Royal Court); *The Comedians* (Oxford Stage Company); *Jump Mr Malinoff, Jump* (Soho Theatre); *Silence* (Birmingham Rep); *La Dispute* (RSC & Lyric Hammersmith); *Angela Carter's Cinderella* (Lyric Hammersmith); *The Woman In Black* (Stephen Joseph Theatre); *Jump To Cow Heaven* (Hull Truck/Edinburgh/Riverside Studios); *The Wasp Factory* (West Yorkshire Playhouse); *Dealing With Claire* (Stephen Joseph Theatre); *A Going Concern* (Stephen Joseph Theatre); *Swamp City* (Birmingham Rep Studio); *Mother Courage And Her Children* (RNT); *Volpone* (RNT). Film credits include *The Altogether* (Establishment Films); *The Hitchhiker's Guide To The Galaxy* (Spyglass/Disney); *Love, Actually* (Duncan Kenworthy); *Ali G In Da House* (Working Title); *Confetti* (Wasted Talent) and *Breaking and Entering*. Television credits include *The Robinsons* (BBC); *Hardware* (Thames Television); *Charles II* (BBC); *Marjorie & Gladys* (Carlton); *Linda Green* (Red for BBC); *The Debt* (BBC); *World Of Pub* (BBC); *Men Only* (Channel 4); *TV To Go* (BBC); *The Office* (BBC).

John Stahl Victor

John's theatre credits include *The Found Man* (Traverse Theatre); *Professor Bernhardi* (Oxford Stage Company); *Tamar's Revenge* (RSC); *Dog In The Manger* (RSC); *Pedro, The Great Pretender* (RSC); *Sergeant Musgrave's Dance* (Oxford Stage Company); *Bread And Butter* (Oxford Stage Company); *Mr Placebo* (Traverse Theatre/Plymouth); *Gagarin Way* (Traverse Theatre); *Crave* (Paines Plough); *The Magic Toyshop* (Shared Experience); *The Weir* (Royal Court); *The Meeting* (Traverse Theatre); *All My Sons* (Theatre Royal, Plymouth); *Two* (Cumbernauld Theatre Company); *Angels And Saints* (Soho Theatre); *Anna Weiss* (Traverse Theatre); *The Jock Stein Story* (Pavilion Theatre, Glasgow); *Shining Souls* (Traverse Theatre); *The Architect* (Traverse Theatre); *Hamlet* (Belgrade Theatre); *Cinderella* (Dundee Rep); *The Real Wurld* (Tron Theatre); *The Crucible* (Lyceum Theatre, Edinburgh); *The Baby* (Tron Theatre); *Paddy's Market* (Tron Theatre); *The Snow Queen* (Lyceum Theatre, Edinburgh); *Death Of A Salesman* (Lyceum Theatre, Edinburgh); *Beneath One Banner* (7:84 Theatre Company); *Sleeping Beauty* (Tron Theatre); *Gamblers* (Tron Theatre); *Macbeth* (Tron Theatre); *Commedia* (Crucible Theatre, Sheffield). Film credits include *Loch Ness* (Working Title). Television includes *The Darien Venture* (BBC Scotland); *Doctors* (BBC); *Murder Rooms* (BBC); *Glasgow Kiss* (BBC); *Doctor Finlay* (ITV); *Resort To Murder* (London Films); *Taggart* (SMG); *High Road* (Scottish TV).

Company

Jonathan Lloyd Director

Jonathan is Associate Director at Soho Theatre where he has directed *Who's Afraid Of The Big Bad Book?*, *Badnuff, Mr Nobody, Modern Dance for Beginners, Julie Burchill is Away, School Play, Jump Mr Malinoff, Jump, The Backroom, Skeleton* and the Under-11s Playwriting Scheme. Further directing credits include *The Backroom* (Bush), *Perpetua* (Birmingham Rep), *Summer Begins* (RNT Studio/Donmar), Channel Four Sitcom Festival (Riverside Studios), *Serving It Up* (Bush), *Blood Knot* (Gate) and *Function of the Orgasm* (Finborough). Writing credits (for children's television) include *Dog and Duck* (ITV) and *You Do Too* (Nickelodeon). Jonathan is currently a Creative Partnerships Fellow on the Clore Leadership Programme.

Jonathan Fensom Designer

Jonathan's theatre credits include *What the Butler Saw* (Hampstead, West End); *Some Girl(s)* (West End); *Talking to Terrorists* (Out of Joint/ Royal Court); *National Anthems* (Old Vic); *Twelfth Night* (West End); *Cloud Nine* (Sheffield Crucible); *Journey's End* (West End and tour); *Abigail's Party* (Hampstead, West End and tour); and *Born Bad* (Hampstead); *East* (Edinburgh and West End); *The Erpingham Camp* (Edinburgh Assembly Rooms and tour); *Alarms and Excursions* (Producciones Alejandro Romay, Argentina); *Richard III* (Pleasance and German tour) and *September Tide* (tour and West End). Jonathan has worked with many of the UK's top producing theatre company's including the National Theatre, West Yorkshire Playhouse, Birmingham Rep, Shared Experience, Royal Court Theatre, Out of Joint, Oxford stage Company, Young Vic, Lyric Hammersmith, Hampstead Theatre, The Bush Theatre and Bath Theatre Royal. Designs for film and Television include; *tvSSFBM EHKL* (Surreal Film) for BBC Arena and costume designs for *Tomorrow La Scala* (BBC films, Director Francesca Joseph), both in 2001. Jonathan was associate designer on Disney's *The Lion King*, which premiered at the New Amsterdam Theatre on Broadway and subsequently opened worldwide. *Abigail's Party* and *Journey's End* were both Olivier Award nominated for Best revival. Forthcoming work includes; *The Knight of the Burning Pestle* (Young Vic); *God of Hell* (Donmar) and three new plays at the National Theatre.

Jason Taylor
Lighting Designer

Jason's credits include *Shoreditch Madonna* (Soho Theatre), *Some Girl(s)* (Gielgud Theatre); *National Anthems* (Old Vic); *Twelfth Night* (Albery Theatre); *Journey's End* (Comedy Theatre and national tour); *High Society* (national tour); *Lady in the Van* (national tour); *Madness of George III* (West Yorkshire Playhouse); *Us and Them* (Hampstead Theatre); *Hobson's Choice*, *Yerma* (Royal Exchange Theatre); *Abigail's Party* (New Ambassadors, Whitehall and national tour); *Pretending to be Me* (Comedy Theatre); *Little Shop of Horrors* (West Yorkshire Playhouse); *My Night with Reg/ Dealer's Choice* (Birmingham Rep); *The Clearing* (Shared Experience);

Single Spies (national tour); *Sitting Pretty* (national tour); *Pirates of Penzance* (national tour); *Office* (Edinburgh International Festival); *Hedda Gabler, Snake in the Fridge* (Royal Exchange Theatre); *The Dead Eye Boy* (Hampstead Theatre) and *Iolanthe, The Mikado* and *Yeoman* (Savoy Theatre). Jason has lit over 200 other productions including 14 seasons at the Open Air Theatre, *Kindertransport* (Vaudeville Theatre); *Rosencrantz and Guildenstern* (Piccadilly Theatre); *And Then There Were None* (Duke Of York's Theatre) and *Great Balls of Fire* (Cambridge Theatre).

Matt McKenzie
Sound Designer

Matt McKenzie came to the UK from New Zealand in 1978. He toured with Paines Plough before he joined The Lyric Theatre Hammersmith in 1979 where he designed the sound for several productions. Since joining Autograph in 1984, Matt's sound design credits include: *Vertigo, That Good Night, Hinge of the World* (Guildford); *The Seagull, A Midsummer Night's Dream, Master and Margarita* and *5-11* (Chichester); *Frame 312, After Miss Julie, Days of Wine and Roses* (Donmar); *Flamingos, Damages* and *After the End* (Bush Theatre); *Iron, People Next Door* (Traverse); and In the West End: *Made in Bangkok, The House of Bernarda Alba, A Piece of My Mind, Journey's End, A Madhouse in Goa, Barnaby and the Old Boys, Irma Vep, Gasping, Map of the Heart, Tango Argentino, When She Danced, Misery, Murder is Easy, The Odd Couple, Pygmailion, Things we do for Love, Long Day's Journey into Night* and *Macbeth, Calico, Wait Until Dark* and *A Life in the Theatre* and for Sir Peter Hall: *Lysistrata, The Master Builder, School for Wives, Mind Millie for Me, A Streetcar Named Desire, Three of a Kind* and *Amadeus* (West End and Broadway). Matt was Sound Supervisor for the Peter Hall Seasons (Old Vic and The Piccadilly) and designed the sound for *Waste, Cloud 9, The Seagull, The Provok'd Wife, King Lear, The Misanthrope, Major Barbara, Filumena* and *Kafka's Dick*. Work for the RSC includes *Family Reunion, Henry V, The Duchess of Malfi, Hamlet, The Lieutenant of Inishmore, Julius Caesar* and *A Midsummer Night's Dream*. Matt's musical work includes *Love off the Shelf* at the Nuffield Theatre; *The Bells are Ringing* and *Talk of the Steamie* at Greenwich; *Forbidden Broadway* and *Blues in the Night* in the West End; Matthew Bourne's *Car Man* (West End and International Tour); *Putting It Together, The Gondoliers* and *How to Succeed in Business Without Really Trying* at Chichester; *Oh What A Lovely War, A Christmas Carol, Sweeney Todd, Merlin and the Winter King* and *Company* for Derby Playhouse and the co-sound design of *Tess* at the Savoy and *Alice in Wonderland* for the RSC. Matt was responsible for the sound design for Soho Theatre's opening and several subsequent productions including *Mr Nobody* and *Badnuff*, also directed by Jonathan Lloyd.

Leann O'Kasi
Assistant Director

Leann's directing credits include *Skinned* (Contact Theatre), *Kriminalz* rehearsed reading (Soho Theatre), *Rose* (C&I Festival), *Haroun and the Sea of Stories* (Co–Dir, Camden Young People's Theatre). Assistant Director: *Macbeth* (Embassy Theatre), *Attempts on Her Life* (Embassy Studio). As a performer, Leann has also trained with Rough Cut Theatre Company and Theatre Venture. Credits include Universal Citizens (Tunisian tour), *Twelfth Night* (AltFest Ensemble), *Hell is Empty* (Stratford Circus). Leann is currently in her third year of a degree in Alternative Theatre and New Performance Practices at Central School of Speech and Drama.

● soho
● theatre

Soho Theatre Company is passionate in its commitment to new writing, producing a year-round programme of bold, original and accessible new plays – many of them from first-time playwrights.

'a foundry for new talent... one of the country's leading producers of new writing' Evening Standard

Soho Theatre + Writers' Centre offers an invaluable resource to emerging playwrights. Our training and outreach programme includes the innovative Under 11s scheme, the Young Writers' Group (15-25s) and a burgeoning series of Nuts and Bolts writing workshops designed to equip new writers with the basic tools of playwriting. We offer the nation's only unsolicited script-reading service, reporting on over 2,000 plays per year. We aim to develop and showcase the most promising new work through the national Verity Bargate Award, the Launch Pad scheme and the Writers' Attachment Programme, working to develop writers not just in theatre but also for TV and film.

'a creative hotbed... not only the making of theatre but the cradle for new screenplay and television scripts' The Times

Contemporary, comfortable, air-conditioned and accessible, Soho Theatre is busy from early morning to late at night. Alongside the production of new plays, it is also an intimate venue to see leading national and international comedians in an eclectic programme mixing emerging new talent with established names.

'London's coolest theatre by a mile' Midweek

● soho
● theatre

Soho Theatre + Writers' Centre, 21 Dean St, London W1D 3NE
Admin: 020 7287 5060 Box Office: 0870 429 6883 Minicom: 020 7478 0136
www.sohotheatre.com email: **box@sohotheatre.com**

The Terrace Bar

The Terrace Bar on the second floor serves a range of soft and alcoholic drinks.

Email information list

For regular programme updates and offers, join our free email information list by emailing **box@sohotheatre.com** or visiting **www.sohotheatre.com/ mailing**.

Hiring the theatre

Soho Theatre has a range of rooms and spaces for hire. Please contact the theatre managers on 020 7287 5060 or go to **www.sohotheatre.com** for further details.

THE SOHO THEATRE DEVELOPMENT CAMPAIGN

Soho Theatre Company receives core funding from Arts Council England, London. In order to provide as diverse a programme as possible and expand our audience development and outreach work, we rely upon additional support from trusts, foundations, individuals and businesses.

All of our major sponsors share a common commitment to developing new areas of activity and encouraging creative partnerships between business and the arts.

We are immensely grateful for the invaluable support from our sponsors and donors and wish to thank them for their continued commitment.

Soho Theatre Company has a Friends Scheme to support its education programme and work in developing new writers and reaching new audiences. To find out how to become a Friend of Soho Theatre, contact the development department on 020 7478 0111, email **development@sohotheatre.com** or visit www.sohotheatre.com.

Sponsors

American Express, Angels, the costumiers, Arts & Business, Bloomberg, Getty Images, International Asset Management, TEQUILA\ London

Major Supporters and Education Patrons

Anthony and Elizabeth Bunker • Tony and Rita Gallagher • Nigel Gee • Roger Jospé • Jack and Linda Keenan • John Lyon's Charity • The Foundation for Sport and the Arts • The Harold Hyam Wingate Foundation

Trusts and Foundations

Anonymous • The Ernest Cook Trust • The Kobler Trust • The Mercer's Company Charitable Trust • The Royal Victoria Hall Foundation • The Paul Hamlyn Foundation • The St James's Trust • Unity Theatre Trust
Dear Friends: Anonymous • Jill and Michael Barrington • David Day • John Drummond • Madeleine Hamel • Michael and Mimi Naughton • Oberon Books • Diana Toeman • Jan and Michael Topham • Carolyn Ward

Friends

Thank you also to the many Soho Friends we are unable to list here. For a full list of our patrons, please visit www.sohotheatre.com

Registered Charity: 267234

BLUE EYES AND HEELS

First published in 2005 by Oberon Books Ltd.
521 Caledonian Road, London N7 9RH
Tel: 020 7607 3637 / Fax: 020 7607 3629
e-mail: info@oberonbooks.com
www.oberonbooks.com

A catalogue record for this book is available from the British Library.

ISBN: 1 84002 638 3

Cover photograph by Hugo Glendinning

Printed in Great Britain by Antony Rowe Ltd, Chippenham.

for Maddy

Thanks firstly to Mike and Nicola at the Bush for their patience and goodwill.

A lot of people took the time to read early drafts and offer suggestions and criticisms, and to all of them, thank you. Especially Bernie, who said, 'that scene with the producer, that works the best, you should make the whole thing about that'.

Thanks as always to Cathy and Phil at ICM for their unstinting support; to Abigail and all at Soho for saying yes, and a manly nod to Jon Lloyd because he's excellent and wasn't put off first time around.

I should also pay special thanks to Martin, for being as good a friend as he is an actor and for championing the play in a way that went far beyond the call of duty.

And finally, to Helen. To whom, quite simply, I owe everything.

Characters

VICTOR
55

DUNCAN
33

EMMA
44

The following script went to press during rehearsals,
and may differ slightly from the play as performed.

On the screen we are watching the last ever ITV Wrestling broadcast, from December 1988.

KENT WALTON: Welcome, grapple fans, for the very last time. Saying goodbye is always sad, but today's sadness is eased a lot by being able to turn back the pages of Wrestling's thirty-three year history on ITV, and enjoy some of the all-time greats. None greater, in my opinion, than the fabulous George Kidd. More of him later. Remember Oddjob? The Great Togo? Wrestling fans knew him before James Bond. Well, today we can offer you the outrageous Adrian Street, Les Kellett, the tough guy who never failed to make us all laugh. Billy Two Rivers – the greatest Red Indian ring warrior of them all... Those were the days of spectacular days at the Royal Albert Hall – royal patronage you notice, with McManus and Pallo in their heyday, and the best seats costing a princely ten guineas. Ricki Starr will parade his unique talents for us later. But notice further down the bill, a heavyweight spot featuring a rising star who really did reach the top of the pile – the late great Mike Marino, the man who taught me so much about the ins and outs of the game. Let's enjoy him now as he faces John Kowalski from Portsmouth... Johnny Kwango's trademark was his famous head-butt. Dangerous when roused, you might say. And certainly he was by Bobby Barnes, who began with his usual peacock style display... We've seen those shoulder straps before, but never that front of the trunks... And so I'm afraid it's goodbye to all that, grapple fans, and as I say 'have a good time' for the last time, I can't do better than to leave the final words to my good friend from Birmingham, the giant bomber himself, big Pat Roach:

PAT ROACH: I think today is a very, very sad day in history, that is the history of Wrestling, that has been in our parlours for many, many years now. How many years Kent? Twenty?

KENT WALTON: More than that.

PAT ROACH: More than that. More than twenty years. And I feel that the Wrestlers would like to say collectively, and I'm sure Caswell Martin will endorse me here now in the ring, that we are very very very sad that in the near future we will no longer be in your front parlour.

Fade.

Scene 1

Music: the overture of the Toreador song from 'Carmen'.

Lights snap up to reveal a wrestling ring. In it stands VICTOR, in full costume. Mask, cape, white flouncy shirt, leggings, wrestling boots and plastic cutlass, a shoulder bag at his feet. Also in the ring, pointed at VICTOR, is an expensive looking digital camera set up on a tripod, connected to a TV. VICTOR looks meekly about him, shifts nervously. DUNCAN strides in. He is fashionably dressed in combat trousers, etc. He carries an orange plastic chair and briefcase. He stops when he sees VICTOR.

DUNCAN: There's no need to stay in costume. You can get changed if you want.

VICTOR: I thought you might like to see it close up, get the full effect.

DUNCAN: Right… The thing is, the cameras are quite far back, you see.

VICTOR: I know, it's just, there are details, on the cutlass and stuff…

DUNCAN: We've got three wide-angle set-ups from the balcony –

VICTOR: ...a galleon...

DUNCAN: – and two hand-helds roaming the aisles. The audience wouldn't get to see you this close up. Even the people in the *hall*.

VICTOR: I know where the cameras are.

Beat.

DUNCAN: Well, maybe you could take your mask off. It's like talking to a... It's very difficult to talk to.

VICTOR: Oh... Sorry...

VICTOR fumbles the mask off as DUNCAN clambers into the ring with his chair.

DUNCAN: I don't think Darren knew what hit him.

VICTOR: (*Modest.*) Well...

DUNCAN: I'm serious. You should see some of the guys we've brought in.

VICTOR: No, he's a nice lad as it goes, we had a chat... I hope you don't mind, I showed him a couple of moves. Nothing flash, just some holds.

DUNCAN: His face. He was like 'Shit!'

The mask is off. DUNCAN simply stares in disbelief.

Shit.

VICTOR: ...What...?

DUNCAN: You're... How old are you?

VICTOR: Fifty-five.

DUNCAN: (*Appalled.*) *Fifty-five?* Did your agent put you on to us?

VICTOR: Don't have one. It was Bob Healy, he –

DUNCAN: You're one of *Bob's*? Oh for fuck's... Did anyone know about this? Did Scarlet know?

VICTOR: Scarlet?

DUNCAN: (*Jabbing his finger to a seat outside the ring.*) She sat there. Pregnant. Sandals.

VICTOR: I don't know.

DUNCAN: Oh this is beautiful...

The temperature suddenly seems to have dropped a couple of degrees.

VICTOR: Um, is he around? Mr Healy.

DUNCAN: What? No. There's a big meeting today. It's just me.

VICTOR: Oh. Right. No, that's fine.

DUNCAN: I mean, didn't you think to *say* anything?

VICTOR: Who to?

DUNCAN: I don't know, *us?* The *girl*, the girl on the desk who buzzed you *up?*

VICTOR: ...What would I have said?

Another awkward pause.

VICTOR fidgets, helpless, lost.

Angry, weary, DUNCAN looks at his watch.

DUNCAN: Okay, let's do this. (*Calling off.*) Emma! (*Sits.*) And there are no other chairs, okay?

VICTOR: Not to worry. Bags of energy, that's me. Some people can play the piano, I've always had bags of energy.

DUNCAN: I've said something. I don't know how many times.

VICTOR: Not to worry. Really.

DUNCAN: (*Standing up to kick his chair.*) I mean look at this. There's a twelve foot *Mondrian* in the boardroom and six different types of biscuit, you'd think they could stretch to some proper – Even Anne Frank had *chairs*.

EMMA appears at the door.

Could you get me a coffee?

A pointed look from EMMA, DUNCAN grudgingly turns to VICTOR.

Look, do you want one? We don't normally offer the…

VICTOR: Er, yes, most kind.

EMMA: How do you like it?

VICTOR: White. Er, milk. Tea.

DUNCAN: Do you want to write that down?

EMMA: I think I'll be okay. I mean, I might have to pop back and check, but I'll give it a shot.

She turns to go.

DUNCAN: Emma… What's going on out there?

EMMA: Right now? Mitchell just did a huge burp so all the men are high-five-ing each other.

DUNCAN: No, I mean – any smoke?

EMMA: Smoke.

DUNCAN: From the chimney.

EMMA: What chimney?

DUNCAN: The *pope's* chimney.

EMMA stares at him blankly.

(*Christ's sake.*) Any *news?*

EMMA: Oh, *news.* No, no news. Bob nipped out to the toilet at one point –

VICTOR chuckles fondly. DUNCAN and EMMA look at him.

– but other than that they've only just started, really.

DUNCAN: Why?

EMMA: They're doing a conference call with Richard and it's about seven in the morning over there.

DUNCAN: So what's everyone else doing? You all just waiting?

EMMA: No, everyone's just getting on with their *jobs,* Duncan.

DUNCAN thinks about this. It sounds like a good idea. He nods.

DUNCAN: Good plan. (*A glance at VICTOR.*) Yeah, that'd look good.

EMMA shakes her head and goes.

DUNCAN looks at VICTOR. He even manages a smile.

Sooooooo. Victor. Victor Victor Victor. Ironically, I was very impressed. No, it's a shame because I particularly liked all the, uh, all the *business* when you came in. The cloak, the shirt, the music. That's exactly the sort of thing we're trying to get our boys to think about. Lots of…*stuff* like that.

VICTOR (*Proud.*) Always caused quite a stir in the halls. Some places, Lancaster, Plymouth, I'd have smoke as well. I asked if you had a smoke machine here and they said no. I thought maybe I could set fire to something, but they said there're alarms and stuff.

DUNCAN: You see, that's what I'm talking about. Gimmicks.

VICTOR: Well, I wouldn't really describe it as a gimmick. It's more like you're telling a *story* –

DUNCAN: In the States they've got it down to a fine art. Everyone's got a gimmick, an angle. I got these tapes out, you should see them. They've got undertakers, psychotics, there's one guy without a leg –

VICTOR: (*Tactfully.*) I've seen them.

DUNCAN: Take Darren for example. Dashing Darren Holmes. He's going to be our centre-piece, we're going to make Darren a superstar. Have you got grandkids?

VICTOR: I've got a son. He's fourteen.

DUNCAN: You wait, a year from now, Darren will be everywhere. Your boy, he'll have Dashing Darren action figures, lunchboxes, dashing Darren duvet covers –

EMMA re-enters with the coffees.

– maximum publicity, maximum profile. The kids will love him, the mums, we'll all love Dashing Darren.

EMMA passes the drinks up through the ropes. While he's stooping VICTOR gives a strange, polite, little bow/bob. EMMA laughs.

(*Languid, showing off a little.*) Bet you could show us a thing or two, eh Emma?

EMMA: (*Turns.*) What?

DUNCAN: Just, you know, I bet you could show us a thing or two. *A couple of holds.* What do you think, Victor?

VICTOR: Ngh.

EMMA: I have no idea what you're talking about. Did you tell Dashing Darren he was getting a car home?

DUNCAN: No, why?

EMMA: He's waiting in reception.

DUNCAN: Isn't someone coming to pick him up?

EMMA: At the moment he's reading the Guardian Media Section upside down.

DUNCAN: (*Panicking now.*) Oh, fuck, this is – Look, I didn't, because they're being really fascist about the taxi account at the moment –

EMMA: (*Sighs.*) I'll talk to him –

DUNCAN: Yeah, but he can't go home on his own, he'll get lost, look what happened last time.

EMMA: It's fine, it's fine, he can call his dad.

DUNCAN: Well, judging from past –

EMMA: I'll dial it for him.

DUNCAN sighs, hugely relieved.

DUNCAN: (*To VICTOR.*) I tell you, we'd be *lost* without this little lady. She's our *mum.*

EMMA: I'm not your mum.

DUNCAN: And she's doing a degree!

EMMA: (*To VICTOR.*) Open University.

DUNCAN: Hey. That's nothing to be ashamed of.

EMMA: I'm not.

DUNCAN: (*Laughs.*) Listen to her. We argue all the time, but it's fine, we love it, don't we.

EMMA: (*Flat, to VICTOR.*) Sometimes I have to pinch myself.

DUNCAN: She says that, I think she's planning something. I think she's going to creep into my flat while I'm asleep one night with a hammer or something.

EMMA: You needn't be asleep.

DUNCAN laughs, loving the banter.

EMMA goes.

DUNCAN: Isn't she great? Diabetic. *Sooooooo.* Let me tell you a bit about the company. Richard, the boss, he's a publisher. Magazines mainly. Er, 'colour' magazines. When I joined six months ago, they were working on ideas aimed at the more, ah, adult market. *Entertainments.* There was a quiz show called 'Strip Poker', topless cooking, dating games –

VICTOR: Topless cooking?

DUNCAN: It sounds great in theory, doesn't it. But the girls wanted to wear aprons, particularly when frying stuff and, well, that sort of defeated the object... Anyway, that's when Bob had his Epiphany. How do you combine all the best elements of Sport, Show Business and Glamour? *Wrestling!* And that's where I came in.

VICTOR: You were in the Wrestling?

DUNCAN: No, I was a researcher on 'Who's That Dog?' It was a panel game, did you see it? Tuesdays at midday. Contestants had to guess the celebrity owner of a given dog. So, okay, the Wrestling. We want to take it right back to its roots: blue collar and proud of it. Straight talking and hard working. Not so much the sport of kings as the sport of the *citizens.* With the right handling, we think wrestling could be The New Football. A working-class religion, everyone with their own favourite, their *idol*, who they follow through triumph and disaster, victory and defeat –

VICTOR: They're not going to be shoots, are they?

DUNCAN: What, photo shoots?

VICTOR: No, 'shoots', it's a – it means genuine fights. Because that's a wholly different skill, that's –

DUNCAN: Oh, no, it's – no, I'm glad you asked me that. No. The fights are decided, who wins who loses, on a *popularity basis.* Whoever's the most popular wins more fights…*i.e.* whoever's selling the most merchandise. You want your hero to do well? Then get out there and buy a duvet cover! It's an Interactive Meritocracy. (*Off VICTOR's look.*) I know. I can't believe no one's thought of it either… And we've got a great team so far. An *Axis* of entertainment. Darren you know about, then there's 'Armageddon'! 'Manson'! 'StormTrooper'! 'The Atrocity'! We've got this Indian guy from Reading, 'Pain-Wallah'! My idea, that one…

VICTOR: It was very kind of you to think of us as well, The Old Guard.

DUNCAN: Listen, I get paid to sit here whatever. It was Bob wanted to see all *you* guys. It's been like 'Driving Miss Daisy' in here…

VICTOR: (*Shifts.*) Well, I know he's always been –

DUNCAN's phone is ringing. The theme tune of 'The Simpsons'. He holds up his hand for VICTOR to stop speaking while he looks at the caller identity. VICTOR obediently does so. DUNCAN lets it ring twice more then answers.

DUNCAN: Yes? Mm-hm? *What?* But the order went in two *weeks* ago… So I'm stuck with – (*Standing up to kick his chair again.*) – some orange thing from a library, sitting there like a tit. Oh, this is classic… So? I only *want* one. *What? Why did Scarlet get it?* Oh cry me a river, she won't *always* be pregnant. There will come a point when she disappears into her mud hut and *spawns* the bloody – (*Heavy sigh.*) What page?

He makes a meal of opening his briefcase, taking out a thin office furniture catalogue and flicking to a page. He looks at the picture.

Look at that back. That's no good to me, I have a dancer's back. I specifically asked for the 'Solitaire' with variable, lockable tilt action. I have to work, every day I have to meet people and because all I *have* is this orange-plastic-housing-benefit-office chair they have to *stand* and some of them might I add are *Very Elderly*… Well when will they get more in? Christ, I'll look like Stephen fucking *Hawking* by then… Alright, but I want arm rests. Has Scarlet got arm rests? I want arm rests.

He hangs up.

Cock suckers. (*Back to VICTOR.*) So that's phase one. Big launch, merchandise merchandise, household names, big success. Blah blah blah, hooray. Phase two: (*He pauses dramatically.*) female wrestlers. Then, well, I mean, fuck. Richard's got some girls from his publishing days, dressed them in some bits of string. Again, the Americans are there before us, they must eat brains for breakfast those guys… We've got 'Black Lace and Lady Leather', they're a tag team. 'Clarabel the Cannibal', 'Anna Conda', she has a snake. All just waiting in the stable…

VICTOR: It sounds terrific.

DUNCAN: But you're thinking, 'Hang on a minute, Duncan, this is well and good but have you captured the mood of the time, have you captured the *zeitgeist?* (*Strangely defensive.*) Well, actually *Victor*, I think we *have*.

VICTOR: Right. Good. Sorry.

DUNCAN: So fine. We've got the campaign, we've got the venues – we're starting off in Leicester – all we need now is the rest of the wrestlers – Oo, that sounds funny. 'The rest of the wrestlers.' (*Looks at his watch.*) Anyway, we should crack on… (*Shouting off.*) Emma! (*To VICTOR, pointing to the camera.*) You don't mind, do you? I think somebody spoke to you about it on the phone.

VICTOR: Oh, no, yes, that's fine. Me and Rollerball Rocco did a link up from our dressing-room when McManus was on 'This Is Your Life', so I know the drill.

DUNCAN: We just need something about yourself, um, why you got into wrestling and so on. I mean, it's kind of academic in your case, but we're all set up so fuck it…

VICTOR: Surely. Although, if it would help, would you like to punch me in the stomach?

DUNCAN: Er, I'm alright, thanks.

VICTOR: Have you got a wardrobe? I could lift it above my head.

DUNCAN: Mmm. It's – No.

EMMA comes in carrying a fold-up garden chair.

You sort Darren out?

EMMA climbs into the ring.

EMMA: His dad's on his way.

DUNCAN: (*The chair.*) Where did you get that?

EMMA: I brought it from home.

DUNCAN sneers covetously at the chair.

EMMA opens it up and places it in front of the camera for VICTOR and crosses to the camera.

All set?

EMMA switches the camera on. VICTOR's face flickers onto the screen.

VICTOR: Oh look.

EMMA: (*To VICTOR.*) Set?

VICTOR: What? Yes. (*The chair.*) And much obliged.

DUNCAN: So if you could just tell us your name.

VICTOR: Victor Sands.

DUNCAN: And your character name.

VICTOR: The Count of Monte Cristo.

DUNCAN: (*Slightly cheesy interview voice.*) That's great. Okay, so, Victor, can you tell us, how did you get into wrestling?

VICTOR: Right. Well. I was five when it started on the telly. I grew up watching it. Every week, there we'd be, me and dad, 'Put the Wrestling on!' Um, dad had been in the war. And afterwards he was a bit poorly. He saw some things, he… Dad was a hero. He was one of the troops that liberated Belsen. Well, the second or third lot in. He said it was… On civvie street he was a postman for God's sake and there he was, seeing these things… But we'd watch the Wrestling and afterwards we'd have a rough and tumble in front of the fire. It – I never got to touch him any other day of the week. He had a beard by now. Mum would get cross, say he'd let himself go. Even though this was ten, eleven years after he got back, he still – I mean this was before anyone had *heard* of counselling –

29

DUNCAN: Victor…

VICTOR: Sorry?

DUNCAN: Sorry, more wrestling, less Belsen…?

VICTOR: Oh right, sorry!

DUNCAN: Sorry, it's just –

VICTOR: No, that's fine, sorry.

DUNCAN: Thanks, Victor.

VICTOR: So. Yes. The Wrestling. Never wanted to do
anything else. I was pretty good at football, mind. Had
a trial for Spurs boys but didn't turn up. No, this was it.
I'd go and see matches with mum. She saw I was getting
a bit obsessed and I think she wanted to put me off, so
one time after a match she goes up to this wrestler, The
Marauder, and says, 'My son thinks he could have a go,'
and The Marauder says, 'Well tell him to come down
to Lincoln's gym in Bromley Sunday morning, we'll see
if he's got anything.' I was, what, about thirteen. I walk
in, there's The Marauder, only he's in his shorts now,
and two others. Well, they just made mincemeat out of
me. (*Chuckling.*) The pain! They tied me in knots, those
lads. I was all over the shop. The next day, I couldn't
eat a sandwich! But I thought, 'Blow this, I'm going
back next week.' And do you know what happened?
Exactly the same thing. And the next week. And the
week after that. I think after a while they were worried
about how much blood I was losing, so showed me a
couple of moves, and that was that – I was off! The first
few years were tough though, no argument, and it was
a bit lonely if I'm honest, coz mum was a bit requisite
with her support. Dad would come when we were
nearby, but mum never really got the gist. It wasn't like
being an apprentice on any other job, there wasn't any
'go and ask for a long stand'. They'd hold me down

and pour sweat in my mouth, go to the toilet in my kit
bag. One time they hung me upside down in a shower
and I passed out for a bit. They wanted to see how
much I wanted to do it… I showed them… I started
off, I was Apollo, I had gold boots and a bed sheet.
Then I was Johnny Bolshevik, I'd come in with a big
coat, and sometimes I was the Masked Marvel when
the Masked Marvel was doing a match somewhere else
or at a wedding or something. And that's when I had
the idea for the Count. (*Laughs.*) The funny thing is, I
never intended to be a villain. In books he's a hero. I
just liked the idea of this chap who goes around from
hall to hall, righting wrongs, punishing the bad, then
disappearing into the night. A mysterious stranger. And
the mask was crucial. I thought the audience would
be able to relate to it, I could be anyone, their dad, an
employee, their teacher, they might have sat next to me
on a bus, 'Who is he?' But they misconstrued me. I'd
climb into the ring and they'd start booing. It was the
mask, they thought I was a Heel. I didn't know what to
do. I was working for Billy Guiver productions at the
time and he said I shouldn't complain, everyone loves
a villain. I said about it being inappropriate for the
name and he said they'd already printed two hundred
posters, so I'd have to keep the sodding name and that
was that. (*Smiles.*) The truth is I've grown quite attached
to it over the years… But you see, telly, that was the
Holy Grail. It was the shop window. You got yourself a
name on telly you'd be top of the bill in Manchester, a
thousand people. It was – I can't explain, when we were
on 'World of Sport', it was *massive.* This is what people
forget. Everything stopped at four o'clock. Shops would
empty. And we were the Robert Wagners. All those big
personalities, heroes and villains, an event every week,
it belonged to everyone, *we* belonged to everyone…

Someone pops their head through the door and signals to EMMA. She checks the camera is running okay, climbs down through the ropes and exits through the doors. DUNCAN watches her suspiciously.

VICTOR is scratching his head, what else can he talk about?

As for now…still touring the halls. The audiences aren't what they were. Ever. But occasionally there's matches abroad. Hamburg… Barcelona… (*Grins.*) Actually that was terrific. It was Olympic year. We missed the games proper but did get a week of the paraplegics. Plus I do a bit of PR on the side, for a company. Meeting and greeting. Um, some acting. Um. Don't drink 'cept my son's birthday, don't smoke, never have… Um, sorry Duncan, I think that's me really.

DUNCAN: Hmm? No, that's fine.

VICTOR: Is there anything else – ?

DUNCAN: I think we've covered pretty much –

VICTOR: I tore my costume once!

DUNCAN: Another time. Now, to finish off, could you give us a bit of a growl?

VICTOR: …A growl?

DUNCAN: And a threat.

VICTOR: A threat?

DUNCAN: We're going to have this thing, 'Next week on The War Zone' and *whoever* growling and issuing a threat.

VICTOR: Right.

DUNCAN: Do you want to jump straight in?

VICTOR: Sure sure. Um.

VICTOR prepares himself.

Right. Grrrrrr.

DUNCAN: Yes… Try again.

VICTOR: Grrrrrrr!

DUNCAN: Mm. Once more? Like a lion.

VICTOR: (*A huge and genuinely terrifying roar.*) *Grrrrrrrrrrrr!*

Beat.

DUNCAN: Right. Bloody hell. Try the threat.

VICTOR: Um…

DUNCAN: Something like 'Dashing Darren! So you reckon you're the boss, well I got news for you pal, *I'm* the boss, *me*, the Count of Monte Cristo, and I'm gonna tear you a new ass!'

VICTOR: Right. Yes. God.

DUNCAN: Give it a go.

VICTOR: Uh. 'Darren. You think you're in charge, however I think you'll find – '

DUNCAN: No, it's got to be –

VICTOR: ' – and I'm going to thump your – '

DUNCAN: No, it's got to be more – you've got to call him names. 'You're a *loser!*'

VICTOR: 'You're a *nancy!*'

DUNCAN: 'You're a *cripple!*'

VICTOR: 'An *idiot!*'

DUNCAN: Um, we try not to use the word idiot with Darren…

VICTOR: 'You're a *clown*!'

DUNCAN: More!

VICTOR: Clowns?

DUNCAN: No –

VICTOR: A monkey!

DUNCAN: A monkey?

VICTOR: 'You're a *monkey!* I'm going to…kick your… neck…off!'

Pause.

DUNCAN has his head in his hands. He rubs his eyes with the balls of his palms.

EMMA re-enters.

EMMA: They're out.

DUNCAN: (*Head snaps up.*) What?

EMMA: Someone wants my chair. The meeting's finished.

VICTOR hops up and immediately starts trying to fold EMMA's chair up for her.

DUNCAN: You're kidding. Does Phil know?

EMMA: I would imagine so. He had his ear pressed against the door at the time, so when they opened it he fell onto the floor.

EMMA climbs up through the ropes to help VICTOR with the chair, DUNCAN sidesteps in front of her.

DUNCAN: (*Anxious, flustered.*) What's – what did they – do you know what they – ?

EMMA: Phil will tell you.

DUNCAN: Phil will tell me *his* version.

EMMA: What about Victor?

DUNCAN: Who's he going to tell? Look at him.

EMMA: I *meant* it's a bit *rude*.

DUNCAN: He's fine.

EMMA: (*Sighs.*) There's going to be a shake up.

DUNCAN: Oh God.

EMMA: This is according to Bob.

DUNCAN: Oh God.

EMMA: Richard wants to restructure the whole UK wing. Sarah's going to join him in South Africa. Mitchell's taking over 'When Plastic Surgery Goes Wrong', and they're looking for someone to co-produce 'The War Zone' with Bob.

VICTOR is still struggling with the chair.

That's fine, I've got it.

VICTOR: 'When Plastic Surgery Goes Wrong'?

EMMA: Everything you need to know is in the title. Sadly.

DUNCAN: And whose decision will that be?

EMMA: What?

DUNCAN: Whose decision will that be? Who gets the promotion.

EMMA: Bob Healy's, I suppose.

DUNCAN: (*Lost in thought.*) Bob Healy…? *In*teresting…

EMMA: (*To VICTOR.*) I'm sorry about this –

DUNCAN: I need to talk to Phil.

EMMA: I don't know where he is.

DUNCAN: Tell him to wait in his office.

EMMA: (*Sighs – to VICTOR.*) Nice to meet you.

EMMA clambers out of the ring and exits as DUNCAN hurriedly starts to gather up his things.

Victor. It's been great.

VICTOR: Is there anything – ?

DUNCAN: No, we're done here.

VICTOR: Well, thanks ever so –

DUNCAN: Someone will be in touch. You can find your way to the dressing-room?

VICTOR: Oh yes, I think –

DUNCAN: Great stuff.

VICTOR: I've really enjoyed –

DUNCAN: Me too.

VICTOR: And if you could give my regards to Bob.

DUNCAN: You bet.

VICTOR: I'm sorry I didn't get a chance to see him. He *said* he might be busy…

DUNCAN starts clambering out of the ring with his plastic chair.

DUNCAN: Yeah, well, y'know: *Television.* It's all kind of… We've… All the time there's something needs… It's really… You know, pressures… 9/11…

VICTOR: We're going fishing at the weekend, we'll catch up then.

DUNCAN: No doubt. Thanks, Victor.

DUNCAN goes.

VICTOR sighs. Beat.

DUNCAN comes back again.

Fishing?

VICTOR: Brighton.

DUNCAN: …Fishing?

VICTOR: (*Confused now.*) …Brighton?

DUNCAN: I didn't realise you…*knew* Bob…

VICTOR: Bob? (*Laughs.*) Oh, I've known Bob for donkeys. He's been coming to the Wrestling since the seventies. Can't remember how we got talking… But no, we used to see no end of each other. His wife Esther and my Carol got quite pally as well. We were – it was ever so sad, we were going to be godparents to their little Nicky, but he had Down's and they didn't want to make a fuss. No, all this, bringing the Wrestling back, he's been talking about it for years. We were always saying, 'Come off it Bob,' but blow me if he hasn't done it! No, Bob likes his fishing. We listen to Radio Four, put the world to rights… Anyway. I'll let you get on.

DUNCAN's phone starts ringing again.

They look at it.

DUNCAN turns it off.

DUNCAN: No hurry.

VICTOR: Oh. Right you are.

VICTOR smiles benignly, as DUNCAN fidgets, desperately trying to think of something to say.

DUNCAN: So… Hmmmmm… Ughhh… I'm a twin!…
Uh… Bleurgh… Hmm… Ah! Wrestling! … Yes, remind
me, when did they take it off? Ninety…?

VICTOR: Eighty-eight. The eighties.

DUNCAN: Bloody Thatcher!

VICTOR: Actually it was Greg Dyke. He'd just taken over
at 'World of Sport' and he thought wrestling was too
down-market for ITV.

DUNCAN: For *ITV?* Jesus, what were you *doing* on there?

VICTOR: We just felt so let down, it was just so sudden.
What always gets forgotten is the public have a *right* to
their Wrestling. One man made that decision for twelve
million people. That's not – that's *Hitler.* You can't just
– it was people's *livelihoods.*

DUNCAN: (*Nodding vigorously.*) Mmm mmm.

VICTOR: And what do they put on instead? These
programmes, these 'up-market' programmes. You see
these people *degrading* themselves, all that squawking
and leering, where's the nobility gone? When they talk
about sex, it's all – Has sex *changed* or something?

DUNCAN: Oh Victor, is this you talking, or me thinking
out loud?

VICTOR: When I was growing up there was subtlety,
there was *charm* and *innuendo.* 'Is this Cockfosters?' 'No,
my name's Miller.'

DUNCAN: It's disgusting, isn't it.

VICTOR: There was *whimsy.* Now it's all… 'flaps' and –

DUNCAN: It's not clever –

VICTOR: It's just nasty –

DUNCAN: *But…* when they get something *right* –

VICTOR: Well, *then* –

DUNCAN: Like, I don't know –

VICTOR: 'Rawhide'.

DUNCAN: – *then* it's –

VICTOR: Well, it's –

DUNCAN: – stuff like *that* –

VICTOR: – gives you faith –

DUNCAN: And it needn't be rare, so don't let them tell you that. It takes people like you and, well, perhaps I can include myself in that –

VICTOR: Well, of course –

DUNCAN: No, because I'm new to this –

VICTOR: Even so, you're –

DUNCAN: Well, whatever, but I'm determined to make a difference –

VICTOR: I've no doubt you will.

DUNCAN: Well, you're very kind. Because potentially this could be –

VICTOR: It could be –

VICTOR starts to say the word 'frightening', DUNCAN starts to say the word 'enormous'. Half-way through the word they realise what the other one is saying and switch words so that VICTOR ends up saying the last syllable of 'enormous' and DUNCAN finishes the word 'frightening'.

DUNCAN: Yes…

VICTOR: Yes…

DUNCAN: But what else can we do, Victor? We're hooked.

VICTOR: Like beetles tied to a pin.

DUNCAN: For me it's the variety. One week I'm talking to Topol about his dog, the next I'm with Victor Sands, the Count of Monte Cristo! No, this is it. You ever heard the saying: 'The Right Place At The Right Time'? It's here. It's now. It's us. It's Darren. There's something in the air, can you feel it?

VICTOR: I can, yes.

DUNCAN: It's a revolution, and this company is on the front line. Like Trotsky and Lenin at the very *gates* of the Bastille. Off with his head! (*Shaking his fist.*) Oh wrestling, you…

VICTOR: You…

DUNCAN: You…

VICTOR: *Cow.*

They chuckle contentedly.

It's funny, going round the country, on the train, in the Allegro, it used to give me time to think. I'd read as well. I've read all sorts. Books about Churchill, mythology, computers, but mostly I'd just think. See, with the Wrestling, people are always saying, 'It's fixed!' But that's missing the point. No one watches – I don't know – '*Hamlet*' and says it's fixed. It doesn't matter if we know who's going to win, it's how we *get there. That's* the entertainment. People want to see struggle. Even if it's not real, they want to see it because that's what their life is. Only, in life, you go through stuff, and you go through it on your own. You can't always scream, you can't always shout or use your fists. When your wife – you can't fall apart. So you'd go to the Wrestling.

The Greeks understood it. That's why they'd go to their tragedies. To see something...*played out* in front of them, something what's usually private. And the Wrestling was so *simple*. These battles, everything was so basic. And I don't mean it was crude. I mean it was black and white. Good people and bad people, Blue-Eyes and Heels. There wasn't any – you knew if someone was evil coz they had bloody great mask on. (*Laughs.*) You've got me started now.

DUNCAN: No, no, go for –

VICTOR: And the power we'd generate, the the the the *fury*, as we'd control the audience, manipulate them. One minute the hero's got the advantage, then all of a sudden the Heel pulls some stunt, something wicked, and *he's* got the upper hand. And the audience can't do anything! They just have to sit and watch! And they're screaming because they want the ref to stop the fight, just to *look*, but he's not paying attention! It's – I even thought of a name for it. Delicious Agony. Coz that's what it is. The villain's pulling a fast one and the audience can only sit and watch. Do you know what I mean?

DUNCAN: (*Earnest.*) Mmmm.

Beat. VICTOR fidgets, suddenly embarrassed by his passion.

VICTOR: But mainly I'd just read...

DUNCAN: No, it's funny, because you've reminded me of something. Your name. That's one of the things I wanted to talk about.

VICTOR: Oh?

DUNCAN: You see, the audience we're looking to attract, they'd want something a bit more...*accessible*.

VICTOR: (*Lost already.*) Right.

DUNCAN: When you devise a show you have a target audience, a socio-demographic group, or sub-section. You've got your 'A's and 'AB's. They're managing directors, GPs, professionals, people with degrees, that sort of thing. Then you've got your 'C1's and 'C2's. 'C1's are skilled workers, secretaries, carpenters, they read the Daily Mail or The Express. 'C2's, pretty much the same, decorators, electricians, only they read The Sun. Then there's your 'D's, labourers, and your 'E's and 'F's, the unemployed, pensioners, people in wheelchairs. You get the picture. Interestingly there's been a bit of a sea change recently. The 'C1's and 'C2's have expanded. Not only in terms of size but income as well. If you imagine, it used to look like a pyramid, now it's like an onion. What I'm saying is: you'd need a different name. 'The Count of Monte Cristo'. You'd confuse them.

VICTOR: But I've always been the Count –

DUNCAN: Don't get me wrong, I love the mask. *Spooky.* What about 'The Ripper!'? Or 'The Executioner!'?

VICTOR: People know me as the Count –

DUNCAN: 'Monster Man!' 'Elephant Face!' The story could be that you're horribly disfigured. A burns victim! If anyone sees your real face, they vomit.

VICTOR: A burns victim?

DUNCAN: What we're doing here, this is Brainstorming.

VICTOR: It's just, a wrestler's *name* is very –

DUNCAN: (*Inspiration.*) Oh God!

VICTOR: What?

DUNCAN: I've got it! What's the one thing *really* gets those people worked up? *Kiddie-fiddlers.* Oh, this is – Every week, wherever we are, that's where you've been re-housed. We'll bring you in under a blanket, dress up some skinny women as mums, to shout from the audience. Placards: the fun we can have spelling paedophile. You can rub yourself between rounds. 'The Fiddler'! 'Giant Gaystack'! I'm riffing now.

VICTOR: I'm not sure…

DUNCAN: Why not? It's the perfect zeitgeist villain.

VICTOR: It's just, as a *parent* –

DUNCAN: I'm only suggesting a few months, then we ditch it and find something new. That's what's great about TV: something stops working, you get rid of it.

VICTOR: Well…I suppose, if we were *saying* something…

DUNCAN: Hey, we can do that as well. (*Laughs.*) The stuff that goes on behind the scenes. I was thinking this the other day, I was thinking I bet *Jesus* must have performed miracles we never heard about. I mean he was running around for years. I bet there was this guy somewhere, 'I hadn't had a shit for six days before I met Jesus!' And Jesus is like, 'You want to keep your voice down a bit…?' And he's going, 'And then Jesus came and waved his cross and I just had a shit the size of a fucking *jeep!*' And Jesus is saying, 'I also bring people back from the dead, you know…' (*Laughs.*) 'The Miracles They Hushed Up'.

VICTOR smiles politely. The conversation is obviously winding down.

VICTOR: (*Beginning his farewell.*) Right, I should be going. I do a bit of debt collection, and –

DUNCAN: (*Quickly, trying to keep the conversation going.*) Do you know Italy?

VICTOR: Italy?

DUNCAN: My parents had this little place down there. I mean it was nothing, it was barely a cottage, but fuck it, me and my girlfriend of the time, we'd rough it every couple of months. She was an actress-stroke-model, but that's not important.

VICTOR: I've seen it on the telly obviously. Bergerac went there. Although it might have been Greece. And it might have been Lovejoy.

DUNCAN: Well, anyway, just up the way was this little village. Shutters, Catholics, donkeys: just gorgeous. We'd stagger up there, I think they called it The Old Town – remind me later, I'll dig the name out, you should take your grandson – and they'd keep the restaurants open all night, and there are kids and dogs running around, and you've got these little terracotta things with olives in, and – is this just me? – the guy who runs it, they've always got these beautiful daughters. They're, like, fifteen, but you're like *Hello...* No wonder they're always having siestas. And you just think, 'I want to fucking *buy* this place and put it in my garden.' I tell you, those Mediterraneans have got it sussed... (*He laughs and shakes his head.*) God, there I go again, listen to me yakking away. There's something about you Victor, I can *talk* to you, you know what I mean? It – I don't know...you're *chatty*.

VICTOR: Am I?

DUNCAN: Oh yeah, listen, you meet some people, they come in here... But *you?* I can't shut up! No, this has all been... You know what I'm going to do?

He presses a button on the camera, a little disc slides out.

I'm going to show this to Phil.

VICTOR: (*Gasp.*) *You're not.*

DUNCAN: Right now.

VICTOR: *No.*

DUNCAN: Watch me.

VICTOR: God.

DUNCAN: (*Modestly.*) Hey. Listen.

Beat.

VICTOR: Who's Phil?

DUNCAN: He works with Bob.

VICTOR: I thought you –

DUNCAN: I work with Phil.

VICTOR: Oh, right.

DUNCAN: Imagine a tree: Richard, then Bob, then me, Phil and Scarlet.

VICTOR: And Emma?

DUNCAN: Er, different tree. (*Gesturing vaguely to the world outside the door.*) All that's much more… It's probably not even a tree… You haven't met Phil, have you. He's great. He's *gay*, but he's great. Not that you'd ever know, he's very discreet. *EastEnders*-gay. I'm going to show him this. (*Lowers his voice.*) The way it works, I do the interviews, then I get to *recommend* people onto the next stage. Bob stays out of it, bless 'im, he doesn't want to impose. Which is so typical of him. Sure, he'll say 'meet this guy', 'Meet *Victor,*' but he wants me to be impartial – as if I wouldn't – then I choose which ones go Upstairs. I say 'Upstairs', it's actually just across – What I'm saying is: This is going Upstairs.

VICTOR: I don't know what to say…

DUNCAN: Don't get me wrong, it's really early doors. Phil's got to see it, we might even have to send it to Richard, and he's in South Africa.

VICTOR: Oh, no, sure.

DUNCAN: And they might think we're all mad!

VICTOR: Of course.

DUNCAN: 'Get out!' (*Laughing.*) 'You're toast!'

VI CTOR: (*Chuckling.*) Right.

DUNCAN: (*Solemn, beginning his farewell.*) Victor.

VICTOR: Yes.

DUNCAN: It's been great. All that *stuff...* Colour me Ever So Impressed.

They shake hands.

So. Plenty to talk about. On your fishing trip.

VICTOR: (*Heartfelt.*) Thank you, Duncan. Thank you.

DUNCAN: With Bob.

VICTOR: What a day this has been.

DUNCAN: In Brighton.

VICTOR: It means so much, I can't tell you.

DUNCAN: Why so surprised? This is how things happen.

VICTOR: No, sure, but –

DUNCAN: We should get you over for dinner sometime. Throw some pasta at you.

VICTOR: (*Honoured.*) *Really?* That would be terrific.

DUNCAN: Because I thought it was *great.* Just, you know, 'if it all works out'. *I* thought it was great.

VICTOR: And thank you for it.

DUNCAN: *I* did.

VICTOR: Yes.

DUNCAN: Me.

VICTOR: Ngh.

DUNCAN: (*Smiles.*) Enough said.

> *They are still shaking hands. DUNCAN suddenly feigns agony, his hand being crushed.*

Argh! That's some handshake!

VICTOR: Oops. Ha ha. Sorry.

DUNCAN: (*Laughing.*) Don't forget to get changed!

VICTOR: Oh no, wouldn't want to do that!

DUNCAN: 'Mummy, look at the strange man!'

VICTOR: Yes. What?

DUNCAN: Enough of this, my lord. (*Brandishing the disc.*) To Phil!

VICTOR: (*Miming punching his own stomach.*) And you're sure I can't tempt you…?

DUNCAN: Honestly.

> *DUNCAN picks up his chair and clambers out of the ring.*

VICTOR: (*Calling after him, à la Kent Walton.*) 'Have a good week, till next week!'

DUNCAN: (*Didn't understand a word of that.*) Absolutely.

> *DUNCAN exits.*

> *VICTOR is alone. He exhales.*

God.

DUNCAN suddenly reappears.

DUNCAN: (*Laughing.*) Phone!

VICTOR: (*Laughing.*) Oops!

DUNCAN: Forget my *head!*

VICTOR: Right.

DUNCAN grabs his phone and, as he exits, turns and mimes fishing – casting out a line and reeling it back in.

They chuckle.

DUNCAN goes.

VICTOR's chuckling dies naturally away. Alone again, he exhales again. This is all a dream.

God.

Blackout.

Music: theme from 'World of Sport'.

The music slowly fades into the roar of an audience and the barking commentary of an American wrestling match. On the screen we are watching 'WWE Smackdown'. It is 15 May 2003. Baltimore, Maryland. Rowdy Roddy Piper stands in the ring, shouting to the audience that he wants to be the one to unmask Mr America at Judgment Day and to finally get back at Hulk Hogan. Mr America (who looks suspiciously like Hulk Hogan) emerges from backstage waving an American flag, which he hands to a fan in the front row. Mr America yells back, he understands why Roddy Piper has a problem with Hulk Hogan, and he would love to kick Roddy Piper's ass just like his idol did in the past! Roddy Piper points out that Hulk Hogan never beat him for a 1-2-3 pinfall. Roddy Piper starts yelling at the fan at ringside waving Mr America's US flag. Mr America defends the fan, saying that the kid in the front row is what is so great about the United States. Sean O'Haire goes out of the ring to intimidate the fan. Roddy Piper then attacks Mr America. Sean O'Haire gets into the ring and joins in the assault. Roddy Piper tries to rip the mask off Mr America, at which point the fan jumps in the ring to stop him. Sean O'Haire spears the fan as security tries to pull him out. Roddy mounts the fan, slaps him around. In the ensuing struggle Roddy Piper grabs the fan's leg…and pulls it off. The audience scream as Roddy stands there in disbelief holding the artificial leg. Horrified, Sean O'Haire backs out of the ring. As Mr America helps the legless fan (still holding the American flag) to the backstage area, they cut to a commercial break.

Fade.

Scene 2

Music: 'Creep', by Radiohead.

The crunch of guitar that starts the chorus, 'But I'm a Creep, I'm a weirdo. What the hell am I doin' here? I don't belong here.'

About six weeks later. Another wrestling ring, with VICTOR standing in the middle, his kit bag at his feet once again. Only now he has a new character and a new costume. His mask is a bit of sacking, like The Elephant Man's. He wears a deliberately tight see-through pac-a-mac, a Britney Spears t-shirt underneath, manky stained trousers and plimsols. He is every tabloid editor's fantasy of a relocated ex-con child molester. He fidgets.

EMMA enters. She is carrying four plastic covers for the corner posts.

EMMA: There's no need to stay in costume, you can get changed if you want.

VICTOR: (*Lifting the mask half-way up.*) Phil asked me to linger.

EMMA: Phil's in a meeting. Everyone's packing up.

VICTOR: Really? That's odd. Maybe he forgot. I'll wait.

EMMA: (*Kind.*) Why don't you go and get changed, Victor. He might be a while.

VICTOR: I told him I'd wait.

Beat. EMMA shrugs.

EMMA: You can keep me company then.

VICTOR: What are you doing?

She crosses to the ring, passing the plastic covers to VICTOR, so she can climb up. He holds the ropes apart for her. She climbs in and he hands her back the covers.

EMMA: Two of the artistes are walking around in just their pants and all the girls are giggling and shrieking and the wrestlers keep dropping stuff and bending down and showing their arses and all the girls are going mad and I'm standing there with my tits like something out of the National Geographic and I thought I'd come in here before someone gets a punch in the throat.

Beat.

VICTOR: I meant… (*The covers.*)

EMMA: Oh. (*She laughs.*) Oh, sorry. No, it's – they're not coming off quick enough. In the tag match, when Liberal Parent undoes the cover so Benefit Cheat can ping Have-A-Go-Hero into the metal post, the covers aren't coming off quick enough. So they're having a stab at velcro.

VICTOR: Do you know how they do that? The chap being thrown – the Blue-Eye – he's actually running. He's in control, so he's dictating how much impact he gets.

EMMA: Right.

VICTOR: Listen to me, giving our secrets away. (*Laughs.*) What is it my son says? 'If I tell you, I'll have to kill you.' (*Laughs.*) I wouldn't kill you really.

EMMA: I'm pleased.

VICTOR: Where would I hide the body, for one thing?! The river probably. Tie a kiddie's bike round your neck, they'd never find you!

He eventually stops laughing.

Beat.

EMMA goes back to her work.

Bob seemed pleased.

EMMA: I thought he looked exhausted.

VICTOR: (*Lowers his voice.*) Did Duncan say anything?

EMMA: What about? Not to me.

VICTOR: I fumbled a couple of moves. It was the mask, it kept slipping round and I couldn't see.

EMMA: It was just a walk-through for the cameras.

VICTOR: No, I know, but I thought I'd mention it. (*Takes off the mask.*) It probably just needs taking in. (*Whispers, ashamed.*) It came off at one point! I wouldn't want anyone thinking I made a *habit* –

DUNCAN appears in the doorway.

DUNCAN: Shoot me. Please, just somebody *shoot me.*

VICTOR: (*Laughing.*) Look out! It's That Man Again!

DUNCAN staggers in, his hand to his head, as if nursing a crippling hangover.

DUNCAN: (*To EMMA.*) Never go for a drink with Bob and Victor. I tell ya, those boys are *maniacs.*

VICTOR: (*Explaining.*) Bob and I were having a drink, and who should wander in?

DUNCAN: Purely by chance. I was walking past, I saw this pub and thought 'that looks nice', and there they were! I should have turned and *ran.*

VICTOR: It's the third time that's happened, we're quite the little gang now. Anyone would think you were following us!

DUNCAN laughs shrilly.

No, it was nice, we made a night of it.

DUNCAN: (*Suddenly.*) 'Lock up your daughters! – '

VICTOR: (*Creepy, pervy voice.*) ' – And your sons too!'

DUNCAN: (*To EMMA.*) We came up with this last night, it's going to be his catchphrase. (*To VICTOR.*) What was the other one?

VICTOR: 'Show me your Tinky-Winky, I'll show you some Tubby Custard.'

Beat.

DUNCAN: Um, I think we decided we didn't like that one…

VICTOR: (*Nods, serious.*) No.

DUNCAN: What about that barmaid!

VICTOR: Oh, now stop.

DUNCAN: (*To EMMA.*) There's this barmaid –

VICTOR: Don't listen to him –

DUNCAN: – Australian of course, stunning actually. Victor goes to get the drinks and he's like *fifteen minutes.* I go over and he's chatting her up!

VICTOR: We were just talking.

DUNCAN: 'Talking'. Bob wanted to throw the ice bucket over you. Take care, Emma, beneath this polite, charming – the guy's a *hound*.

VICTOR: (*Laughing.*) Don't make me come over there…

DUNCAN: We need to keep you on a *lead*. Get you a bloody *license*.

VICTOR: She missed her mum.

DUNCAN: Take you to the *vet*.

VICTOR: He's being silly.

DUNCAN: (*Struggling to keep the dog theme going.*) …Keep you…away…from cats…

EVERYONE looks at the floor.

VICTOR: So, what do you think of Leicester?

DUNCAN: The hotel's nice.

VICTOR: I've invested in a guide book, been seeing the sights. The cathedral dates back to the eleventh century.

DUNCAN: (*Nudging EMMA.*) So does she! (*He laughs heartily.*)

VICTOR: Duncan. While you're here, quick apology.

DUNCAN: Of course. What for?

VICTOR: I fumbled a couple of moves during the camera test. Nothing drastic, just some holds. I think it was the mask. Perhaps I could have a word with wardrobe? It wasn't because – I am keeping up. I'm down that gym every evening –

DUNCAN: (*Dismissing VICTOR's concerns.*) Hey. Hey.

VICTOR: That said, I did miss last night. I thought I should do a bit of research for my character, so watched 'Bugsy Malone' a couple of times.

DUNCAN: You, sir, are a trouper.

VICTOR: Truth be told, I did think I'd be seeing more of the *other* boys down the gym. I don't know how they're keeping up those physiques, they must train at dawn or something!

DUNCAN: Yeeeesssss, I think, you know, everyone's worked out their own regime.

VICTOR: Even Scott's not there much, and I thought he'd be working flat out now he's in the first show.

DUNCAN: Why? He loses.

EMMA: Scott's in the first show now?

DUNCAN: The climax. Dashing Darren vs Asylum Ali. In the blurb, it's going to say if Ali wins he gets a passport.

EMMA: I thought Darren was fighting Persistent Offender.

DUNCAN: (*Laughs, shakes his head.*) We've got this great gag: Persistent-Offender can't be here as he's been arrested for his hundred and sixty-eighth burglary, and due to ridiculously liberal sentencing has been sent on holiday to the Lake District. That reminds me, can you get a kid with polio?

EMMA: A kid with polio.

DUNCAN: Yeah, it's for Darren, he's going to carry him aloft as he enters the ring. So no fat ones obviously. We don't want one who's turned bitter and, you know, let himself go. Actually, see if you can round a few up. It can be like the Pied Piper, as he led the children to…

EMMA: Their deaths.

VICTOR: No, what I meant was, there's not been much – if I may say so – concentration on *technique*. I said to the trainer I'd be more than happy to take them through some basics, but he just sort of shrugged and said talk to the choreographer.

DUNCAN: Victor. The last thing I want is you worrying about trivialities. I want you *focused*. *I'm* going to talk to her, and say…talk to Victor.

VICTOR: Well, really, that's very kind.

DUNCAN: Scarlet's not been bothering you, has she?

VICTOR: Scarlet? Her without the bra? She's not said a word to me, why?

DUNCAN: She can get a bit clingy. If it becomes a problem, just say the word. Did you get the fruit basket?

VICTOR: Haven't I thanked you? Oh, it's terrific, Duncan.

DUNCAN: No, no, it's fine, I just wanted to check they'd –

VICTOR: (*To EMMA.*) Pears, strawberries, *peaches* – it must be *years* since I had a peach that good!

DUNCAN: I picked them out myself.

VICTOR: I can hardly get into my hotel room now! What with the fruit, the flowers…

DUNCAN: Just a token of… What flowers?

VICTOR: From Phil.

DUNCAN: Phil sent you flowers? He never said.

VICTOR: Lilies, I think. A lovely little arrangement.

DUNCAN: (*Brisk.*) Yeah, well, we have an account with Interflora, it doesn't actually *cost* him anything… (*Low, to EMMA.*) Christ, it's hardly subtle, is it? And let's face it, he's wasting his time. *I* was the one came up with the whole Tabloid Villain thing. What's Phil ever come up with? (*Quickly.*) Apart from that quiz show. So if *anyone's* going to – Fuck it, where is he? I'm gonna – where is he?

EMMA: A meeting.

VICTOR: I'm waiting myself.

DUNCAN: What sort of meeting?

EMMA: I don't know. With Richard.

DUNCAN: What time is it there?

EMMA: In Phil's office? Probably the same time it is in here. He's back.

DUNCAN's face drops.

DUNCAN: *Richard* is?! *Richard*-Richard? Since when?

EMMA: This morning.

DUNCAN: Fuckety-fuck. (*To EMMA.*) Why didn't – ? Christ!

He scrambles out of the room.

VICTOR: Do people still get polio?

EMMA goes back to her work.

Duncan's great, isn't he. Very sharp, very clever. It's nice to see a young chap so full of enthusiasm.

EMMA: He's full of something.

VICTOR: No, this is what we've been waiting for. This is justice. Since word got out I was on board, the phone's been red hot. I'm the ambassador. They're thinking if this goes well, you'll want *all* the old faces back.

EMMA: You must be pretty pleased yourself.

VICTOR: (*Laughs.*) 'Surprised' more like. I thought, 'Look at those dolly fellas. There's no way they'll want you, boy.' Even Bob was taken aback by how positive Duncan was. Any minute now, we thought, they'll be showing me the door. 'Get some toast!'

EMMA is looking at him.

EMMA: Mm.

VICTOR: Punch me in the stomach.

EMMA: Excuse me?

VICTOR: Go on – *Bosh!*

He mimes punching EMMA in the stomach. She flinches slightly away.

Tell you what! We haven't got a wardrobe, so give us a stack of chairs, I'll lift them above my head!

EMMA: Um.

VICTOR: Kent Walton said I was 'vice-like'. The other fella would wear himself out just struggling. Eight, nine, ten, all over. Always looked dead convincing.

EMMA: I'm sure.

VICTOR: Would you like to see some photos?

EMMA tries to think of an objection. She can't. She sighs.

EMMA: Why not.

VICTOR trots to his kit bag and takes out an envelope of photos, there are some yellowing newspaper cuttings in there as well.

VICTOR: I brought them to show Bob, give him a laugh seeing all the old faces… Ah, this was Billingham. Nineteen eighty. That's me on the left, with Freddie Wilson the Butcher of Bradford.

EMMA: So it is – God you were huge! Did you win?

VICTOR: Nearly. Oh you should have seen me. Tall, thick hair, like I'd just stepped out of a catalogue. I'd come in, my big cape, lots of smoke, lots of music, dead exciting. (*A bit of a naughty twinkle, a bit of a naughty wobble of the head.*) Always went down well with the ladies. The various ladies. Ring Rats, we called them. Not always young or good looking, but always there. (*Another photo.*) That's me advertising yoghurt. (*Another photo.*) That's me lifting up a car. (*Another photo.*) That's Preston.

EMMA: You knew Kenny Dalglish?

VICTOR: Eh? No, that's Suzie Mitchell, the Blonde Bombshell. Great mates. I was a natural, they said, coz of my neck. It's all in the neck you see. That's something you can't be taught.

EMMA: Right.

VICTOR: I've always said, put a good wrestler in the ring with a boxer, the wrestler would win. You know why? Because all the wrestler needs to do is get hold of a finger, and the boxer's had it.

EMMA: So the boxer wouldn't be able to wear any gloves.

VICTOR: Well, no, the boxer wouldn't be able to wear any gloves, that goes without saying – But that's all it takes. Just one finger and he's got him. (*Chuckles.*) Don't tell a boxer I told you that!

EMMA: Okay.

VICTOR mimes punching her in the stomach again. Again EMMA flinches away.

VICTOR: And again! *Bosh.* Elbow in the face! She's gone, she's totally gone.

He chuckles heartily.

EMMA smiles thinly.

(*Another photo.*) Alan Dennison. The great. He's dead. (*Another photo.*) Mike Marino. Beautiful wrestler. He's dead. (*Another photo.*) Johnny Kwango. He of the famous flying head-butt. He's dead. (*Another photo.*) Ah, The Creature. He's got a pub in Kettering.

EMMA hands the photos back, but one catches her attention.

Long time ago. I do a bit of public relations work now, for Trimex, you heard of them? They distribute thread.

EMMA: Right.

VICTOR: They're good people at Trimex. And Customers are their Cornerstone. I look after some of their clients on golf days, dinners, lunches, that sort of thing.

EMMA: Were you really famous?

VICTOR: (*Beaming.*) I met Arthur C Clarke. Plus, I do a bit of debt collection for a friend. He has this business, he collects bad debts from all over Essex.

EMMA: You're like a bailiff?

VICTOR: A bailiff? Oh no, nothing like that. It's all very civilised, no nasty stuff. Businesses and factories on the whole. Say you owed my boss ten grand, and you'd ignored all the letters. Well, then I'd pop round to your office in all my gear.

EMMA: No.

VICTOR: Mask, cape, the lot. Always causes quite a stir with the employees.

EMMA: Do they ever think you're a singing telegram?

VICTOR: A singing telegram? No. No, of course not.

Beat.

Sometimes.

EMMA: (*The photo.*) Who's this?

VICTOR: Eh? Oh – That's my son, Jamie. And that arm, that's my ex-wife, Carol.

EMMA: You're divorced? I'm divorced.

VICTOR: There was another man. He bought our Datsun.

EMMA: I'm sorry.

VICTOR: I can't blame her. She had needs and I was at the Fairfields Hall. It was a bomb waiting to happen.

VICTOR runs his fingers over the photo.

You?

EMMA: No, nothing… We just divorced.

VICTOR: I don't see him much. Carol's remarried now, they've got this house, she says having me around confuses things. Plus…I don't know…some things happened. They were getting a lot of dog-mess through their letterbox, so Carol drew a line. Which I didn't think was fair as nobody could prove it was me. (*Grins, conspiratorial.*) But all this has given me a spur. I've got back in touch. I sent him a book token and he rang me! He was a bit – you know what they're like at that age. They just grunt. But then I told him about this and whoosh! 'When's it on? Who've you met?' He's never seen me on telly before, not properly, just tapes. There were some other photos but I threw them off a ferry.

VICTOR puts the photos away. He chuckles.

Freddie Wilson, he had this thing he used to do, he'd – Come here, I'll show you.

EMMA: Sorry?

VICTOR: Come here, I'll show you this thing Freddie
    Wilson did. It was terribly funny.

EMMA: I'm alright, thanks.

VICTOR: It won't take a second.

EMMA: I've got a bit of sunburn.

VICTOR: You started off with the approach. Come at me.

EMMA: What?

VICTOR: Come at me.

EMMA: How?

VICTOR: It – how do you think?

*EMMA looks at VICTOR; sensing there's no way she's going to
get out of this, she sighs and cautiously but unenthusiastically
approaches VICTOR with her arms in a pincer like position.
VICTOR deftly avoids her arms and locks her in a hold.*

Now. We'd start off, something simple, a hold, cheap
and cheerful. Maybe the 'Arm and Neck Hold', also
known as Bulling. You alright?

EMMA: Well –

*As VICTOR talks he gently moves EMMA back and forth, like
a puppet, so she acts out the part of the other wrestler.*

VICTOR: Then one of us might slip into a headlock, the
    old reliable, it's a beautiful move. Lift him up. On the
    floor, *bam!* Up he gets, quick as you like, *woof!*: body
    check. Back I go, into the ropes, use the spring back
    – Hello, what's this? – *Smash!* Now, I'm bigger than
    him so if I come off the ropes he'll know about it, and
    realistically he'll have to sell the move and go down.
    That's when you sort out who the professionals are. You

get some lad, it's his hometown or he's just been on the telly, he won't want to look weak so he won't sell the move. That happens, you might want to give him a little smack, '*Behave yourself!*' With Freddie there was nothing like that. Maybe we'd get a sub-plot going about his back. It's lovely when that happens, coz then every time he goes onto his back you'd get an 'oooh' from the audience. Kent Walton would say, 'The Count's really working on that back of his.' Or say it was a shoulder, *zip!*, into an arm-lock and the audience are all rubbing their shoulders. Anyway, I've got Freddie in an arm-lock – you're so stiff! – but then, quick as you like, he's slipped out and doubled it back on me. Cheeky. A flyweight, some Blue-Eye, they'd do a forward roll or somersault or something flashy. Big chaps, we're a bit more restricted, so maybe I'd stagger down, the ref counts me out, first fall to Freddie. We break, Freddie walks away, arms raised in victory. But look out!: I'm up on my feet, charging towards him. The crowd are screaming at him to turn round, he's saying 'What?' Too late! *Whack*, through the ropes he goes, onto the floor. I get a public warning, he rolls around in agony. Oh, they hate me now. Trick of the trade: as you go down, keep an arm extended and sweep over some chairs, it's just a nice touch...

EMMA: I'm sure. Yes, no, that was very funny.

VICTOR: I haven't got to the funny bit.

EMMA: There's more?

VICTOR: So, I'm Freddie, and he's got me in, say, a Double Waist Lock, and the crowd are really going mad now, and he's whispering in my ear, ''Ere,' he's saying, ''Ere Vic, ask me why I'm so fat,' and I'm saying, 'What?' 'Go on,' he's saying, 'ask me why I'm so fat.' 'I don't know, Freddie,' I says, 'why are you so fat?' 'Coz every time I fuck your missus she gives me a Malteaser!'

I tell you, it's lucky I had a mask on I was laughing that much.

He laughs heartily, then stops, lets go of Emma and steps back.

Oh I'm sorry, I don't like to use dressing-room talk in front of a lady.

EMMA: (*Rubbing her arm.*) That's okay.

VICTOR: (*Grabbing her again.*) So I'd struggle out of that –

EMMA: Oh Jesus.

VICTOR: – and get him into our friend the headlock, and I'm shouting at the crowd, 'What shall I do with him? Shall I break his neck?' Well, they're going bananas by now, chucking things into the ring – no offence but the women were the worst –

EMMA: *Ahhh!*

VICTOR: What's wrong?

EMMA: My back!

VICTOR: What is it?

EMMA: I've hurt my back.

VICTOR: Oh God, come here, sit down, oh God, I'm sorry.

EMMA: *Jesus,* that –

VICTOR: Do you want a glass of water?

EMMA: No, it's fine, just let me lie down for a second.

VICTOR helps EMMA ease herself gently down onto the mat.

Ahhhh!

VICTOR: Oh God.

EMMA: Honestly, it's fine.

VICTOR: Are you okay? Oh God, I'm sorry.

EMMA: Don't worry about it –

VICTOR: I just wanted to tell you about the Wrestling. They were such good times, Emma.

EMMA lies on the mats, stiff as a board, as if lying in state. VICTOR stands over her awkwardly.

Should I get someone?

EMMA: No.

VICTOR: You might just need clicking.

EMMA: I'll be fine, just let me lie here.

VICTOR: Is there anything I can do?

EMMA: When I get up, is the offer still open to punch you in the stomach?

VICTOR stands and fidgets. He still doesn't know what to do.

Tell you what, shall I have a pop at these covers?

EMMA: You don't need to do that.

VICTOR: I don't mind. Bags of energy, that's me. Some people can play the piano, I've always had bags of energy.

He picks up the remaining covers and sets to work, moving around the ring, EMMA still lying flat on the floor.

It's slowing down a bit, to tell you the truth, the Trimex work. They're restructuring their corporate entertainment department. They've got someone used to be on 'Gladiators'. The clients, they're all younger these days, they want someone off the telly from nearly now. I'm still their number two, though! I said to Vincent, some of the old boys, they don't want to deal with anyone else. 'Where's Victor?' they'd say if I wasn't

there. I can work those old boys you see, you don't lose
that, I can work them like a crowd. (*Chuckles.*) There
was this time: Lancaster Civic Hall, me and Jungle Jim
Johnson. I was –

EMMA: Which one?

VICTOR: – Eh?

EMMA: Which Gladiator?

VICTOR: (*Shrugs.*) I don't know their – Tank, is it? Or
Rodent?... Foxy?

Finished, he sits down cross-legged next to her.

Pause.

I'll tell you the worst thing about nowadays. CGI. Back
in the seventies and eighties there was no end of science
fiction on telly. All those shows, there was always a
monster or a robot, always something for big chaps like
me. In 'Blake's Seven' I was this thing in the hills that
kept attacking a village. I'd be done by a computer now.

Beat.

I wish it was back then. Or my father's time and I could
sign up! Going off to war, shoulder to shoulder with
good men. Maybe fight alongside my dad. 'Alright, Vic?
'Alright, Tom?' Even the wars are different now. They've
even taken that away.

Beat.

How's the back?

EMMA: Fine, apart from the searing pain.

VICTOR: We used to get knocked about all the time. I've
had pretty much every bone broken at some point.
Arm, wrist, leg, most of my fingers, half a dozen ribs.
They were your medals. You wore them with pride.

That's what's ironical. There we were, bashing seven shades of daylight out of each other, but if someone got hurt it was usually by mistake!

EMMA: How ironical.

VICTOR: That's the skill, you see. Keeping it safe, but making it look real.

EMMA: You think you do that?

VICTOR: What?

EMMA: There's this chap been thrown into an iron post, he staggers about a bit, then jumps on the other chap's head as if nothing happened. You think that looks real?

VICTOR: What do you want, blood?!

EMMA: No, but realistically –

VICTOR: I told you, I've not exactly been unscathed, thank you very much!

EMMA: No, sure, but *realistically* –

VICTOR: That's where the entertainment comes in.

EMMA: The entertainment. Right.

VICTOR: What you're talking about, that's a street fight. You want a street fight?

EMMA: No, but at least a street fight doesn't… Look, maybe it's me, I just don't see what's entertaining about – I know it's fake, I know no one *really* gets hurt, and that just makes it worse. If you'd ever… I need to sit up. Help me sit up.

VICTOR: Er, is that wise?

EMMA: I want to ask you something.

VICTOR helps EMMA heave herself up.

Have you ever been punched in the face?

She slides back so she's sitting against one of the corner posts.

VICTOR: That's what I'm saying, we were forever
getting –

EMMA: I mean really. With intent.

VICTOR: ...I don't know.

EMMA: Trust me, you'd remember. It hurts, okay? It
really hurts. And you don't get up. You don't get up
for years. And the first time, the surprise. You made a
mistake. That's it. You tripped and fell, cracked your
nose on the wall on your way down. Anything else
seems...impossible. And then it becomes your fault.
Fucking moody cow. (*Looks around.*) This was going to
be temporary. Six years I've been here. The path of
least resistance. And that's what it does. You become
frightened, you become cynical. You go to the shops in
the dark. You wear sunglasses in November. You cower.
You retreat. You shut down. You hide.

She struggles to her feet.

So I'm sorry, but to turn that into a fucking *game-
show*...to take something like – to make it so *puerile*...
What have we become, that we put this on TV? Is this
all we're left with? And I hate that it's just me saying
this! You should see the looks I get out there. Like I'm
pissing on the birthday cake.

Beat.

I should get on. Can't wait to try out those moves on
someone.

She goes back to what she was doing.

*VICTOR fidgets. He picks up his bag, moves towards the edge
of the ring and stops.*

VICTOR: I miss my boy.

EMMA: I know.

VICTOR: When we said goodbye his new dad was there
so we just shook hands. I'm sorry, but that has to be
worth something. And if this doesn't work… If this
doesn't work…

Beat.

VICTOR exits.

EMMA stands for a moment.

DUNCAN comes back.

DUNCAN: You having a little rest?

EMMA: No, I was just – (*She shakes her head, forget it.*) How
did it go with Richard?

DUNCAN: Yeah, pretty good. Well, I mean, disastrously
for – (*Gestures around.*) but no, pretty – (*Can't hold it
back any longer.*) Oh God, it was hysterical. I get there
and the atmosphere is fucking – It's just Richard and
Phil, they're looking at these tapes, and Richard's
fast-forwarding through all this stuff going, 'And what
the fuck is *this?* And what the fuck is *this*?', and Phil's
looking at me like, 'Run, Forrest, run!' So I sit down and
we get to the camera test from today, and by this point
Richard's got his head in his hands, he's like 'Kill me!',
but me and Phil are just looking at the screen, watching
Victor huffing about. Then all of a sudden Richard turns
to us and says 'Guys. I'm not a *expert* on these things…
but to *me* that looks very much like an old man dressed
as a *paedophile.*' Oh God, we all just *pissed* ourselves.
You know when it's really tense, and someone just *says*
something? He's going, 'Bob is bringing us fat old men,
dressing them like child molesters, and we are *filming*
them rolling around in a wrestling ring. I'm not missing

anything *out*, am I?' And we're like, 'We know! We
know!' And by now Richard's got beyond – he's just
laughing. He's like, 'Is Bob *on* something? Should we be
checking the *dosage*?' I'd forgotten how *funny* Richard
can be. Then we dug out the interview – remember
the interview? – oh God, we had to stop the tape twice,
Phil had coffee coming out of his nose. 'My dad was in
Belsen so I became a wrestler.' Priceless.

EMMA: Why was he so surprised? He must have seen the
tapes.

DUNCAN: Not the new stuff, not till two days ago. That's
why he's back. He hit the roof. In South Africa. Got the
next flight out.

EMMA: What's he going to do?

DUNCAN: He's going to talk to the network, see if we can
get transmission put back a few weeks while we *try* and
sort this mess out. (*Sighs.*) No, Bob's really lost the plot.
It's a shame but hardly surprising, the man's sixty if he's
a day. Knowing where you were when Kennedy was
shot is not something to be proud of in television.

EMMA: What are you talking about?

DUNCAN: (*Grins.*) He's being put out to grass. He's
getting his clock. Richard thinks his talents would be
best served elsewhere. Like in his living-room, waiting
for meals-on-wheels.

EMMA: But why? What's Bob got to do with it?

DUNCAN: (*Sings.*) 'What's *Bob*, but a secondhand
emotion?' (*Clears his throat in the ensuing silence.*) Bob
landed us in this.

EMMA: How?

DUNCAN: *Victor*, for one thing. Plus the villains, the
tabloid villains. It was all his idea.

EMMA: No, it wasn't, it was your idea!

DUNCAN: Um, *no*, it was Bob's.

EMMA: It was yours!

DUNCAN: Hey, I was only *Associate* Producer, I couldn't just *plough on* – stuff had to be *agreed.*

EMMA: Bob may have sanctioned it, but it was still *your* idea.

DUNCAN: No, it was Bob's.

EMMA: It was yours! You *told* everyone it was yours!

DUNCAN: What I *said* –

EMMA: You've been bloody –

DUNCAN: – see, the thing about television –

EMMA: – you've been dining *out* – !

DUNCAN: (*Angry.*) Look, the chances are Bob would have thought of it eventually!

EMMA: …So that's it? He's just going?

DUNCAN: Why so surprised? This is how people go.

EMMA: So who's the producer now?

> *DUNCAN grins.*

> Oh God.

DUNCAN: (*Barely containing his delight.*) I got it! I fucking *got it.* I cannot *wait* to see the look on Phil's face. Cunt. And Scarlet. Her and her 'back to work in just three weeks'. Yeah, it was probably the kid's idea. Sick of the sound of her chanting…

EMMA: And what about Victor?

DUNCAN: Well, quite. Poor old Victor, he'll be devastated. *Bloody Bob! (Solemn, humble.)* I just hope he can understand it's for the good of the show…

EMMA shakes her head and laughs emptily.

EMMA: The show. Yeah, I'm sure that'll be a great comfort. God forbid anything should stop us producing this mixture of porn and the shopping channel.

DUNCAN: *(Correcting her.)* Uh, this 'interactive meritocracy'.

EMMA: *(Gathering up the post covers.)* Duncan, I know to get through the day everyone has to spend a big portion of it pretending all this is worthwhile, but please, just for a second, can we stop pretending we work for the Red Cross.

DUNCAN: You think *this* isn't worthwhile?

EMMA: *(Turns.)* You think it *is?*

DUNCAN: Of course.

EMMA: No, but really.

DUNCAN: Yes!

EMMA: *(Hushed.)* I won't tell anyone.

DUNCAN: I do!

EMMA: *(As if just hearing he has a terminal illness.)* Oh my God. I'm so sorry, I had no idea.

DUNCAN: What, what's that supposed to mean?

EMMA: I just, all this time, I thought you were, you know, I thought you were just saying telly stuff. I didn't realise you *believed* it.

DUNCAN: Hey, this is a great show!

EMMA: It's cynical, it glorifies violence, it's demeaning, it's about two steps away from televised executions. I don't understand, Duncan. You're not stupid, you could make anything you wanted, and you do *this?*

DUNCAN: Yes. I do this.

He laughs, a little exasperated, disbelieving.

I hate this assumption that *your* idea of entertainment, of what's good, this narrow little furrow, this niche, this corner, that *this* should be the benchmark. That the tastes of a tiny insignificant few should determine everything else. The snobbery of it, the arrogance. How dare you. Why *isn't* this quality broadcasting? Who decided *your* taste was really so much better? When did tacky become tacky? It's like you see this line, this direct link between your tastes, your sensibilities and, what, Shakespeare? The Greeks? (*Laughs.*) It's such bullshit! You know where that line leads? Me. Here. Us. This. Entertainment, my friend.

EMMA: No, because something happened along the way. Back then it was about something bigger, something greater. This is just degrading.

DUNCAN: In your eyes maybe, but it's What The Public Wants.

EMMA: No it isn't!

DUNCAN: What, do you really think on some council estate somewhere, there's this teenage mum, sat in front of a TV, fourteen mixed-race kids round her ankles, saying to herself, 'When-oh-when will they serialize The Brothers Karamazov?' You want to know who's responsible for the dumbing down of television, look outside the *Fucking Window*! They don't watch 'You've Been Framed' with a *gun* at their head, they don't even watch it because there's nothing else *on* – they watch it because they're thick as pigshit with an almost orgiastic enjoyment of other people's failure and discomfort! This image you have of them, I don't know where you get it. Most of the public still point at planes, but oh no, you dress them up, you imbue them with refinements and tastes like yours. It's vanity. And patronage. It's like putting glasses and a bonnet on a cat. 'Ah, but if only they were given a *chance...*' They don't *want* a chance, they want blood, tits and beer. 'Mummy, why are your hands so soft?' 'Because I'm fucking *twelve.*' Televised executions? Fuck, bring it on, I'll put in a pitch. Dancing girls and fireworks, out-take compilations and roll-over weeks, I'll give you the greatest show on earth. And if I don't, somebody else will. Not because we're diseased sadists, but because The Public Would Demand It. They'd be all over that like fat bridesmaids. If it makes it easier, tell yourself it's all a conspiracy. That we're working night and day to suppress Merchant Ivory. Even as we speak, hordes of road-sweepers and check-out girls from Argos are planning to storm broadcasting house, *demanding* an Eisenstein retrospective. The thing is, I gotta tell ya, it just ain't true. We don't set the standards, we're just the good and faithful servants attending to the whims of our masters. It's so *easy* to blame us, so much more comforting than admit they *are* different, they *are* stupid and violent and frightening and, at the end of the day, you really wouldn't want to live *next door* to the public.

EMMA: And it's so much easier to strip everything down to its lowest common denominator and say 'it's what they want' than do something good.

DUNCAN: Millions Of Viewers is what *makes* something 'good'.

EMMA: When did *that* happen? There used to be a difference between 'good' and 'popular', when did *that* change? Did I miss a memo or something?

DUNCAN: If it doesn't have an audience, it's nothing. It's indulgence, it's a hobby.

EMMA: That's *one* criteria.

DUNCAN: It's the *only* criteria!

EMMA: Something that makes people's lives *better*, then.

DUNCAN: This *will* make people's lives better, you fucking snob, just not yours. *You* are a minority now. Your opinion is becoming less and less important every day. Middle-aged and middle-class. The Ringo Star of demographics. It's a young man's game now.

EMMA: What is?

DUNCAN: *Everything is!*

Silence.

EMMA: So what made you think, even for a minute, they'd really want Victor? They'd want *any* of that stuff?

Beat. DUNCAN thinks about this. He shrugs.

DUNCAN: It could have been the right decision. I didn't know. No one knows anything any more…

EMMA: But what did *you* think?

DUNCAN: …I'm not sure I follow.

EMMA: When you saw Victor, for the first time, before anything happened, what was *your* opinion?

DUNCAN frowns, concentrating, as if trying to remember the name of the boy he sat next to at infant school. Eventually he gives up.

DUNCAN: I don't see how this is important.

EMMA: (*Weary, almost imploring.*) Because that's all that's left. If there are no rules any more, then all you can rely on is your own taste, your own...*integrity*.

DUNCAN: What is the big deal about 'integrity'? No, I'm serious. What is this *fear* about losing it? It's the twenty-first century equivalent of virginity. You ask me, 'integrity' is just something people wheel out to defend failure.

EMMA: Because if you haven't *got* it, if you don't actually know what you *think* without somebody telling you first, without being focus-grouped or looking at a fucking *chart*, you're...nothing. You're...you're a *zero*. You're like that man in the rhyme, 'yesterday upon the stair I met a man who wasn't there'.

DUNCAN: Having no integrity isn't like missing a *kidney*, okay? I've stood in Don Estelle's living-room taking Polaroids of his dog. Believe me, to get through a day like that the last thing you need distracting you is *integrity*.

EMMA: Then, Christ, we really might as well shut up shop now, because that really is it. We really are the last generation. There will be no more great women and men, no one of principle. Nothing good ever came from being this fearful. Nothing good has ever come from wanting to be popular.

Beat.

DUNCAN: I don't know if you ever saw, there used to be this show on TV, 'The Great Egg Race'. What it was, they'd have teams, and they had to build a little thing, a contraption, out of straws and cups and sellotape and stuff, and it had to carry an egg, like, the length of a table. Typical fucking *English* programme. So anyway, my grammar school, they decide to have a go. Just, you know, a little project for everyone, end of term. So I built this thing. And it was – the principle was really simple. I stuck two cups together at the bottom and got these straws and poked them through so they were like an axel, and tied another load of straws to one end so it was like an L shape. Then I attached an elastic band to the other end and to the inside of the cup and wound it round and round and round. And what it did, the bit of the axel that's sticking out, that would drag along the ground and keep the axel still, so when you let it go the rubber band would unwind and propel the thing along. And it won! Well, it didn't actually win, *none* of them fucking, but at least mine *moved.* And my teacher was like, 'This is really clever… You could be an engineer…' And he was right. But instead I… I'm not stupid, I know what this job is. I know what it's done. Swallowed up a whole generation of engineers, teachers, doctors, scientists, activists, nurses, fathers, mothers… All of us fighting for the same scrap of land, all of us trying to *justify* –

EMMA: It doesn't justify –

DUNCAN: It has to.

EMMA shakes her head, makes to leave. DUNCAN sidesteps, blocking her path.

But what have you brought to show the class, mm? You know your problem? You're a spectator. You bitch and whine, but that's it. You're still here, Emma! In our hall, on our wages, you're still here! It does rather undercut your argument. An opinion is no good unless you do something with it.

VICTOR appears in the doorway. He is dressed normally now.

VICTOR: I thought I'd say cheerio.

EMMA: Victor...

DUNCAN: Oh Christ...

VICTOR: I hope you don't mind, I heard voices and waited for a pause.

DUNCAN: Yes, right, cheerio.

VICTOR: (*Reaching up through the ropes to shake hands.*) Thanks again, you know, for everything.

DUNCAN: Pleasure. There's a people carrier going back to the hotel in five minutes, you might want to –

VICTOR: Oh, yes, right-you-are. (*Shaking hands with EMMA.*) And it was lovely talking to you. (*To DUNCAN.*) She's a lovely lady, I hope you all know that. Solid gold.

DUNCAN: We should have her melted. Adieu.

VICTOR: I've got such a good feeling about this.

DUNCAN: We're going to make lots of noise.

VICTOR: You know when you can just – ? It's like a smell. The smell of success.

DUNCAN: Well, let's hope so. (*Indicating the door.*) They're usually very prompt –

VICTOR: (*To EMMA, chuckling.*) I drive him mad! 'Stop talking, Victor!'

DUNCAN: Don't be silly.

VICTOR: He says that. You wait, when I've gone: 'Aarrgghh!' (*Chuckles.*) No, I'll see you tomorrow.

VICTOR gives a cheery salute and starts off towards the door.

EMMA: Victor.

He stops.

Duncan's been promoted, he's a producer now.

VICTOR: *No!*

DUNCAN: Oh, I'm sure Victor doesn't / want to hear –

EMMA: Amongst other things he's in charge of casting now.

VICTOR: Good Lord.

EMMA: Hiring and firing. Sorry, isn't that what we were just talking about?

DUNCAN laughs, a bit shrilly – 'shut up!'

VICTOR puts his bag down by the door and returns to the ringside.

VICTOR: (*Solemn.*) May I be the first to offer my congratulations. In fact – no, stay there. (*He climbs into the ring.*) May I?

He hugs DUNCAN.

DUNCAN: (*From somewhere in VICTOR's chest.*) 'In charge' is a tad – 'a greater say' is more –

VICTOR: I can't say I'm surprised. I knew you were destined for great things, I said as much to Emma.

DUNCAN: – Richard still makes the final decisions –

EMMA: He's being modest. He was just telling me all his plans.

VICTOR: No, I can spot talent a mile off. You'll change the world, young man, I have no doubt.

DUNCAN: Ngh.

EMMA: Well, I'm sure you've got lots to talk about…

DUNCAN: What? You're going where are you going you can't go.

VICTOR: (*To EMMA, beginning his farewell all over again.*) It was lovely talking to you –

DUNCAN: (*To EMMA.*) Look, things got said, but let's not lose sight – (*Desperate.*) Who do you think'll get hurt the most from this?

EMMA: Oh, I've got a pretty good idea... Victor, when you're done, there's a little café across from the entrance, come and talk to me.

VICTOR: Uh, sure...

EMMA: Just, you know, if you want to.

DUNCAN: (*Hissed.*) Ask if they're taking anyone on at the moment.

EMMA: Will you come and talk to me, Victor?

VICTOR nods/shrugs – okay.

You were right, Duncan, thanks. I enjoyed that.

She climbs out of the ring and starts towards the door. DUNCAN runs to the ropes and shouts after her

DUNCAN: Hey, Emma.

She stops.

You didn't do that for him. Never tell yourself you did that for him.

Beat.

She goes.

DUNCAN turns to face VICTOR. It's just the two of them now. They chuckle. VICTOR politely, DUNCAN uneasily.

VICTOR: So. Richard.

DUNCAN: Yeeeeess…

VICTOR: Is he pleased?

DUNCAN: Um, I'll be straight with you Victor… What we have here is a conflict of *interpretation*… The thing is, our boys need to have a certain *look*. You've seen those Americans. Let's face it, they're gorgeous.

VICTOR: I don't understand.

DUNCAN: Hey, me neither. This whole Body Fascism thing makes you sick, doesn't it. But what do I know? The world's fucked up: fact. You ever seen a homeless Chinese person? *Exactly*. What's that about?

VICTOR: But –

DUNCAN: We have certain obligations. To advertisers, to networks, to…the list goes on. We have to *Attract a Subsection*. Remember the onion? Well, we *want* that onion. But to *get* that onion we have to make tough choices, and *like* an onion, it might make us cry…

VICTOR: What onion?

DUNCAN: Look. Christ. Look. Richard saw the tape. And he just felt for the sake of the sponsors we needed something a bit more…a bit less…a bit more…*energetic*.

Beat.

VICTOR: I'm out, aren't I.

DUNCAN: Demographically –

VICTOR: (*Suddenly animated.*) Where's Bob Healy?

DUNCAN: (*Moving away, carefully keeping VICTOR on the other side of the ring.*) Bob's a traditionalist. Don't get me wrong, we all love Bob, this whole thing – but when you're devising a show you have to think of the *long game*.

They start circling the ring.

VICTOR: You said you thought I was great…

DUNCAN: And I did.

VICTOR: You sent me fruit, and flowers…

DUNCAN: I only sent the fruit.

VICTOR: And now you just…like I'm some…

DUNCAN: I know it's tough –

VICTOR: …some piece…a…

DUNCAN: You think I'm happy doing this?

VICTOR: You don't know what this means…

DUNCAN: What can I say? My hands are tied.

VICTOR: I told you about my dad…

DUNCAN: And I really enjoyed it.

VICTOR: (*Anguished.*) You gave me *hope*. You gave me *hope*.

DUNCAN: (*Almost offended.*) If I've *ever* given hope it was *entirely* unintentional –

VICTOR: *Bastard!*

VICTOR suddenly lunges at DUNCAN, who darts out of the way.

DUNCAN: (*Running around the ring as VICTOR pursues him.*) It was Richard! I tried to talk him round but he wouldn't listen! He said it was obscene, I said it was retro!

VICTOR: Making me listen to your clap-trap, you're a prize shit, son –

DUNCAN tries to dive under the ropes. VICTOR catches him, yanks him back and gets him in a headlock.

DUNCAN: Oh God oh God let me go oh God let me go Victor.

VICTOR: You want a growl, I'll give you a growl alright –

DUNCAN: I'm ordering you to let me go.

VICTOR: I'm gonna bloody break you, son.

DUNCAN: Don't make me call someone because make no mistake I will.

VICTOR: (*Yelling, as if to a packed arena.*) What shall I do with him?! *What shall I do with him?!*

DUNCAN: (*Going purple.*) You, my friend, are about to discover a World Of Pain…

VICTOR hip-throws DUNCAN onto the mats, he lands with a thump.

VICTOR drops on him, pinning DUNCAN to the floor.

VICTOR: Give me your finger, give me your bloody finger!

DUNCAN is trying to crawl away, out from under VICTOR.

DUNCAN: Oh please oh God oh fuck –

VICTOR: Once you've got a finger, that's *it* –

DUNCAN: Help! I'm being attacked by The Fiddler!

VICTOR fumbles away at DUNCAN's hand.

DUNCAN manages to wriggle out from under him and starts to crawl away, but VICTOR grabs his ankle, yanks him back and locks him in a 'leg split'. DUNCAN's right arm is pinned under him, VICTOR grips his left, leaving DUNCAN's face wide open for VICTOR to strike. DUNCAN cowers, waiting for the blow. VICTOR goes to hit him, but stops. They stare at each other, panting.

What…?

VICTOR: I should…

DUNCAN: …what…

VICTOR: What's wrong with me…?

DUNCAN: Uh…?

VICTOR: …this is…

DUNCAN: Victor…please…

VICTOR: I should make you beg…

DUNCAN: We can – there's lots of stuff to talk about, there's commentary, we can talk about that…

VICTOR: This is… What…

DUNCAN: Come on now, let's…

VICTOR: …what have you done to me…?

DUNCAN: (*Extricating himself.*) That's it…

VICTOR: Time was, I could have…

DUNCAN: I don't doubt it.

VICTOR: I could have…

DUNCAN: There we go…

VICTOR: I don't understand…

DUNCAN is free now. But he doesn't run. He looks down at VICTOR sat on the mat, breathing hard.

What's wrong with me…? …I should break you, son…

DUNCAN: Yeah. Well. You had your chance. That was your chance.

DUNCAN crosses around VICTOR, leans over the ropes and peers out through the door.

Lucky for you I don't think anyone heard. I have to *work* here, this is… Get your breath back. You had a turn. You had a turn and fell over, okay? Christ, I should call the FUCKING POLICE.

VICTOR doesn't move, still breathing heavily.

Come on, get your breath back. Your bag's by the door.

He looks down at VICTOR, still bowed and wheezing on the floor.

Are you done now? Fuck's sake. Are you done now?

Blackout.